T0155582

Modern CSS

Master the Key Concepts of CSS for Modern Web Development

Joe Attardi

Apress®

Modern CSS

Joe Attardi
Billerica, MA, USA

ISBN-13 (pbk): 978-1-4842-6293-1
https://doi.org/10.1007/978-1-4842-6294-8

ISBN-13 (electronic): 978-1-4842-6294-8

Managing Director, Apress Media LLC: Welmoed Spahr
Acquisitions Editor: Louise Corrigan
Development Editor: James Markham
Coordinating Editor: Nancy Chen

Cover designed by eStudioCalamar

Cover image designed by Freepik (www.freepik.com)

Distributed to the book trade worldwide by Springer Science+Business Media New York, 1 New York Plaza, New York, NY 10004. Phone 1-800-SPRINGER, fax (201) 348-4505, e-mail orders-ny@springer-sbm.com, or visit www.springeronline.com. Apress Media, LLC is a California LLC and the sole member (owner) is Springer Science + Business Media Finance Inc (SSBM Finance Inc). SSBM Finance Inc is a **Delaware** corporation.

For information on translations, please e-mail booktranslations@springernature.com; for reprint, paperback, or audio rights, please e-mail bookpermissions@springernature.com.

Apress titles may be purchased in bulk for academic, corporate, or promotional use. eBook versions and licenses are also available for most titles. For more information, reference our Print and eBook Bulk Sales web page at http://www.apress.com/bulk-sales.

Any source code or other supplementary material referenced by the author in this book is available to readers on GitHub via the book's product page, located at www.apress.com/9781484262931. For more detailed information, please visit http://www.apress.com/source-code.

Printed on acid-free paper

To Liz and Benjamin – you are my whole world.

Table of Contents

About the Author

 **Joe Attardi** is a software engineer specializing in front-end development. He has over 15 years' experience working with JavaScript, HTML, and CSS and has worked extensively with front-end technologies such as Angular and React. He currently works at Salesforce and has worked in the past with companies such as Dell and Nortel. He is also the author of *Using Gatsby and Netlify CMS*, an Apress title. He lives in the Boston area with his wife and son. You can find him on Twitter at @JoeAttardi.

About the Technical Reviewer

Alexander Nnakwue has a background in Mechanical Engineering from the University of Ibadan, Nigeria, and has been a front-end developer for over 3 years working on both web and mobile technologies. He also has experience as a technical author, writer, and reviewer. He enjoys programming for the Web, and occasionally, you can also find him playing soccer. He was born in Benin City and is currently based in Lagos, Nigeria.

Acknowledgments

I'd like to start by thanking my wonderful wife, Liz, for her constant love and encouragement throughout the whole writing process – and for understanding when I locked myself away in solitude to write. And my little toddler, Benjamin, for giving me much-needed breaks from writing for play time.

Thanks to all my friends and family for always supporting and encouraging my interest in computers and technology.

This book began its life as a self-published work, and I'd like to thank Apress for making it what it is today. I'd also like to thank the awesome team at Apress – Louise Corrigan, Nancy Chen, and Jim Markham – for guiding me through the process every step of the way. I appreciate their patience with me as a first-time author.

Thanks to Alexander Nnakwue, the technical reviewer for this book, for his time and excellent feedback, helping make this book even better.

Special thanks also to Stephanie Eckles and Ellie Baker, two extremely talented CSS experts who reviewed some of the chapters in the previous, self-published version of this book.

Introduction

In this book, we will take a tour of modern CSS. Whether you're brand new to CSS or you have some experience and need a refresher, this book will have something for you.

However, this book will not teach you color theory or good design techniques. The intent of this book is to give you a strong foundation with the various CSS technologies.

In Chapter 1, we'll start at the very beginning and talk about what CSS is and how it works. We'll explore the DOM, the CSSOM, and the render tree as well as take a quick detour to look at CSS preprocessors (though we won't cover them further in the book).

In Chapter 2, we will tackle CSS selectors. These are critical to understand. Selectors determine what CSS styles are applied to what elements. We'll also explore the concept of specificity.

Once we've laid the groundwork, we'll start to talk about CSS concepts in Chapter 3 like the box model, units, colors, and overflow. We'll also look at CSS custom properties, better known as variables.

We'll finally start applying styles in Chapter 4, where we'll look at borders, box shadows, and opacity. We will see several ways to hide an element on the page.

In Chapter 5, we'll learn all about backgrounds and gradients (which are actually a type of background image).

Chapter 6 deals with the important topic of styling text. We'll learn about text styles and layout, as well as how to use web fonts.

We'll see how to lay out and position elements in Chapter 7. This covers the different positions such as `static`, `relative`, `absolute`, `fixed`, and `sticky`. Also, in this chapter, we'll see the topic of stacking contexts and Z-index, which often trip up even experienced developers.

In Chapter 8, we'll cover CSS transforms. This allows you to apply transformations such as rotation, scale, and skew to elements. We'll also see a few examples of creating shapes with CSS.

Transforms can be combined with transitions, which is one topic of Chapter 9, to create all kinds of interesting effects. Transitions can be applied to transforms or a slew of other CSS properties. Chapter 9 also covers animations, which takes the concepts of transitions to the next level.

Chapter 10 is dedicated to the flexible box layout, or flexbox, which is a powerful one-dimensional layout tool that has excellent browser support. With flexbox, we can finally easily center a `div`!

Chapter 11 is a gentle introduction to responsive design techniques. While it is not an exhaustive guide – entire books have been written on the subject – it lays a good foundation, covering topics such as media queries and fluid typography.

Finally, we save the best for last. Chapter 12 is all about CSS Grid, the latest and greatest layout tool in the CSS toolbox. It doesn't have great Internet Explorer support, but all of the other major browsers have full support for it.

In Chapter 13 we'll see some other topics for further learning, such as CSS methodologies like BEM and OOCSS, as well as utility-first CSS and Houdini, the future of CSS.

Let's get started!

CHAPTER 1

Introduction to CSS

Chances are that you already have *some* idea of what CSS is, or else you probably wouldn't have been interested in this book. But let's start at the beginning, to make sure we're all on the same page.

CSS stands for Cascading Style Sheets. It's a language for specifying how an HTML document is displayed. Without CSS, every website would just be Times New Roman with tiny buttons. It's capable of much more than styling text, however. CSS lets us define entire layouts and position elements and even perform animations.

Style sheets are self-explanatory, but what is a *cascading* style sheet? Because more than one style rule could apply to a given HTML element, there needs to be some way to determine which rule should apply in the event of a conflict. The styles "cascade" from less specific to more specific selectors, and the most specific rule wins. Specificity is an important concept in CSS, and we will discuss that in more detail later.

A bit of history

Before CSS, support for styling in HTML was limited. The style information was included in the HTML markup. For example, the font face, size, and color were specified with the font tag and several different attributes, as shown in Listing 1-1.

Listing 1-1. Styling HTML with the font tag

```
<font face="Arial, sans-serif"
      color="blue"
      size="12">
  Hello world!
</font>
```

© Joe Attardi 2020
J. Attardi, *Modern CSS*, https://doi.org/10.1007/978-1-4842-6294-8_1

This resulted in a tight coupling between the semantics and the presentation of a document, which made websites harder to maintain. There were some basic layout options, such as the center tag. For more advanced layouts, the only real option was to use HTML tables. Tables were meant to display tabular data. One disadvantage of using tables for layout is that someone using a screen reader will have a very hard time navigating the page.

There were several other proposals for style sheets for HTML documents as well, but CSS was first proposed at a conference in Chicago in 1994. The following year saw the birth of the World Wide Web Consortium (W3C), and the initial version of the CSS standard was published in late 1996. In the years since, CSS has evolved into a powerful tool for styling HTML documents.

Anatomy of a CSS rule

A CSS style sheet consists of rules. CSS rules target HTML elements by using selectors that describe the elements to which the styles should be applied. As we will see later, elements can be selected in many ways.

Rule syntax

A rule consists of a selector followed by a block of CSS properties contained inside curly braces. The properties consist of a property and value separated by a colon and are delimited with semicolons. A value may be a single value or a collection of multiple values, depending on the property.

Every element in the document that is matched by the selector has the properties in the CSS rule applied to it. An example of a CSS rule is shown in Figure 1-1.

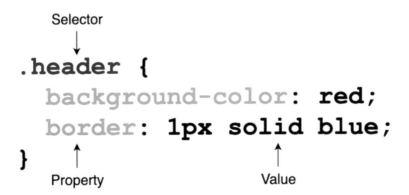

Figure 1-1. *The structure of a CSS rule*

This rule targets any element with the class header (more on classes later). Any element with this class will have a red background and a 1-pixel solid blue border.

In the previous example, background-color and border are CSS *properties*. The border width is specified as 1px. px is a CSS *unit*. There are many units including em, rem, and %. We will learn more about the different CSS units later.

Property conflicts

If the same property is used more than once in a given rule, the last definition in the rule wins. An example of this is shown in Listing 1-2.

Listing 1-2. A CSS rule with conflicting properties

```
.header {
  background-color: red;
  background-color: blue;
}
```

In Listing 1-2, the element with the class header will have a blue background because it is the last one in the rule. The second background-color property overrides the first.

Comments

CSS can also contain comments, inside and outside of rules, as shown in Listing 1-3.

Listing 1-3. A CSS style sheet with comments

```
/* This is a comment outside of a rule */

.header {
  /* This is a comment inside of a rule */
  background-color: red;
}
```

At-rules

An *at-rule* is a special CSS rule that acts as a directive controlling the behavior of CSS. It is called an at-rule because it starts with the "at" sign (@). Here are some examples of at-rules:

- `@charset`: Defines the character encoding used in the CSS file.

- `@import`: Imports, or includes, the contents of another style sheet.

- `@media`: Defines a media query. We will cover media queries in Chapter 11.

- `@keyframes`: Defines a set of keyframes for a CSS animation. Animations will be covered in Chapter 9.

How CSS is used

There are several ways to use CSS in an HTML document. They all have the end result: a style sheet that is applied to the document.

Inline styles

Every HTML element supports the `style` attribute. Inline styles are specified as CSS properties in the value of the `style` attribute. An inline style does not contain selectors or curly braces; it is simply a collection of CSS properties. An example of an inline style is shown in Listing 1-4.

Listing 1-4. An element with inline styles

```
<div style="background-color: red;">
  Hello world!
</div>
```

The element in Listing 1-4 will have a red background. The properties specified in an element's inline style will apply to that element only. If there are conflicts in the rules that apply to an element, its inline style always takes precedence. For example, if there was a CSS rule somewhere that made all div elements have a blue background, this element's inline style would override that and give it a red background.

Style blocks

CSS rules can also be specified inside a style sheet within the HTML document itself. This is done by adding CSS rules inside of a `style` element. Style blocks are typically added to the document's head element. These are full style sheets with selectors and rules. Listing 1-5 shows an example HTML document containing a `style` element.

Listing 1-5. A style block inside an HTML document

```
<!DOCTYPE html>
<html>
  <head>
    <style>
      div {
        background-color: red;
      }
    </style>
  </head>
  <body>
    <div>Hello world!</div>
  </body>
</html>
```

In the preceding document, all `div` elements will have a red background.

External style sheets

Lastly, CSS rules can also be listed in a style sheet file with a `.css` extension. This style sheet is then referenced in the head of the HTML document using a `link` element. In the following example, using the code from Listing 1-6, all `div` elements in the document will have a red background. The linked CSS file is shown in Listing 1-7.

Listing 1-6. An HTML document referencing an external style sheet

```
<!DOCTYPE html>
<html>
  <head>
    <link rel="stylesheet" href="/path/to/file.css">
```

```
  </head>
  <body>
    <div>Hello world!</div>
  </body>
</html>
```

Listing 1-7. A simple external CSS file

```
div {
  background-color: red;
}
```

Browser support

The CSS features discussed in this book are well supported in modern browsers: recent versions of Chrome, Firefox, Edge, and Safari. Some features have limited or no support in older browsers such as Internet Explorer 11. These compatibility issues will be called out where applicable.

Some features are supported but only with vendor-specific prefixes, but this is rare with modern browsers. For example, several years ago, the @keyframes rule (which we'll explore in Chapter 9) was still somewhat experimental, so in order to support it, prefixes had to be used. This is shown in Listing 1-8.

Listing 1-8. Using vendor prefixes

```
@keyframes spin {
  from { transform: rotate(0); }
  to { transform: rotate(360deg); }
}

@-moz-keyframes spin {
  from { -moz-transform: rotate(0); }
  to { -moz-transform: rotate(360deg); }
}
```

```
@-webkit-keyframes spin {
  from { -webkit-transform: rotate(0); }
  to { -webkit-transform: rotate(360deg); }
}
```

The main disadvantage of vendor prefixes is that they require duplication, as shown in Listing 1-8. For each block, the same keyframes have to be specified.

More recent browser versions tend to use experimental feature flags rather than vendor prefixes. These are special configuration flags that are exposed in an advanced configuration interface where experimental features can be turned on and off.

If you still need to support older browsers that use prefixes, there are tools such as Autoprefixer which lets you write prefix-free CSS. The tool then parses the CSS and generates a new style sheet containing the duplicated vendor-prefixed rules and properties.

Web resources

There are many resources and references that are useful when using CSS. Here are a few of the best.

CanIUse.com

The website CanIUse.com (https://caniuse.com) is a great resource for finding out the browser support of a given feature. This site maintains a database of up-to-date browser support information for different CSS features. Figure 1-2 shows a screenshot of an example query.

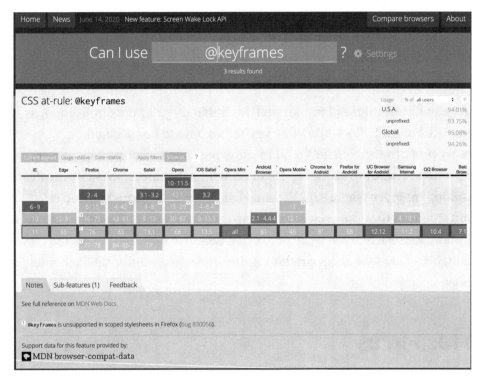

Figure 1-2. *Screenshot of CanIUse.com*

Mozilla Developer Network

Another useful resource is the Mozilla Developer Network (`https://developer.mozilla.org`), or MDN for short. MDN has a complete reference to HTML, CSS, JavaScript, and more. It is an exhaustive reference to all CSS properties.

CSS preprocessors

CSS is not without its limitations and pain points. CSS preprocessors, such as Sass, LESS, and Stylus, provide additional features not found in plain CSS. These tools provide an extended, or even completely different, syntax for writing CSS rules. When you build the application, the preprocessor takes your style sheets and converts them to plain CSS, ready to use in the browser.

We won't cover CSS preprocessors in this book beyond this section, but here is a quick overview if you are interested in using them.

Nested rules

CSS rules don't support nesting. This means that a CSS rule with a selector cannot appear inside another CSS rule. Most preprocessors, however, allow this. For example, the Sass code in Listing 1-9 has nested rules.

Listing 1-9. Nested selectors in Sass

```
.header {
  background-color: red;

  h1 {
    font-size: 24px;
  }
}
```

The inner h1 selector will only match h1 elements that are a descendant of an element that matches the outer rule, which would be an element with the class header. The equivalent CSS for this nested rule would look like Listing 1-10.

Listing 1-10. The equivalent CSS

```
.header {
  background-color: red;
}

.header h1 {
  font-size: 24px;
}
```

Variables

If you are supporting modern browsers, this is not as compelling of a reason to use a preprocessor, because recent versions of Edge, Firefox, Chrome, and Safari all support native CSS variables. However, if you need to support older browsers such as IE11, this can be a useful feature.

In Sass, for example, variables are declared and referenced starting with a $ character, as shown in Listing 1-11.

Listing 1-11. Sass variable syntax

```
$header-color: red;

.header {
  background-color: $header-color;
}
```

Mixins

A mixin allows you to write a set of CSS properties and values, then apply that entire set of properties to another CSS rule without having to repeat all the code. If you have to support older browsers that expect vendor prefixes on some properties, this can be useful.

For example, the Flexible Box Layout Module, or flexbox, is supported on all modern browsers. If you need to support older browsers, they may require vendor prefixes. Your CSS might look something like Listing 1-12.

Listing 1-12. Vendor prefixes for flexbox

```
.header {
  display: -webkit-flex;
  display: -ms-flexbox;
  display: flex;
}
```

The given code will need to be repeated for every element using a flexbox layout. This can be simplified by creating a flexbox mixin in Sass, shown in Listing 1-13.

Listing 1-13. Sass flexbox mixin

```
@mixin flexbox {
  display: -webkit-flex;
  display: -ms-flexbox;
  display: flex;
}
```

```
.header {
  @include flexbox;
}
```

Mixins are very useful for cutting down on duplicated code. They can even take arguments to customize the resulting CSS.

How CSS works in the browser

Now, let's take a look at how the browser renders a page with CSS.

The Document Object Model (DOM)

The Document Object Model, or DOM, is a data structure in the browser. It is a tree of objects that represent the elements in the document and their structure and hierarchy. This tree is composed of DOM nodes. The DOM is created by reading the HTML markup, tokenizing it, parsing it, and finally creating the object hierarchy that makes up the DOM.

Consider the example HTML document shown in Listing 1-14.

Listing 1-14. A simple HTML document

```
<html>
  <body>
    <h1>Hello World</h1>
    <div>
      <h2>Subtitle</h2>
      <p>Hello world!</p>
    </div>
  </body>
</html>
```

The corresponding DOM tree is shown in Figure 1-3.

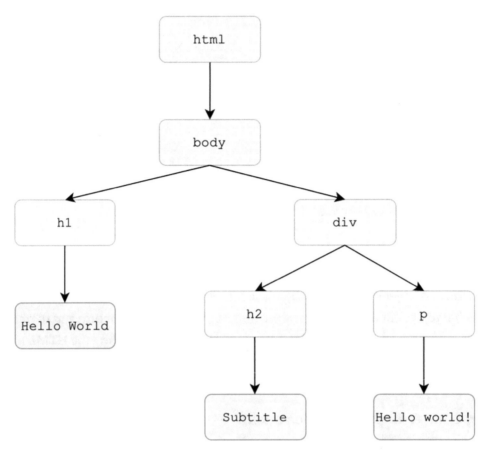

Figure 1-3. *The DOM tree corresponds to the HTML document*

The CSS Object Model (CSSOM)

Similar to the DOM, there is also a CSS Object Model, or CSSOM. This is another tree structure that represents the hierarchy of styles in the document. While they are both tree structures, the CSSOM is a separate structure from the DOM.

Listing 1-15 contains a CSS style sheet meant to be applied to the HTML document in Listing 1-14.

Listing 1-15. CSS style sheet

```
body {
  font-size: 16px;
}
```

```
h1 {
  font-size: 1.5rem;
  color: orangered;
}

div {
  padding: 1rem;
}

div h2 {
  font-size: 1.2rem;
  color: blue;
}

div p {
  font-size: 0.9rem;
  color: gray;
}
```

The browser parses the CSS (which blocks the rendering of the page) and creates the CSSOM. Figure 1-4 shows the structure of the CSSOM tree.

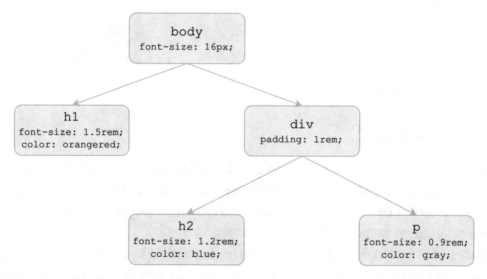

Figure 1-4. *The CSSOM tree*

The render tree

Once the DOM and CSSOM are complete, they are combined to form the render tree. The render tree contains all the information the browser needs to render the page. To do this, the browser calculates which CSS rules apply to which elements in the DOM.

Figure 1-5 shows the render tree resulting from combining the DOM and CSSOM trees.

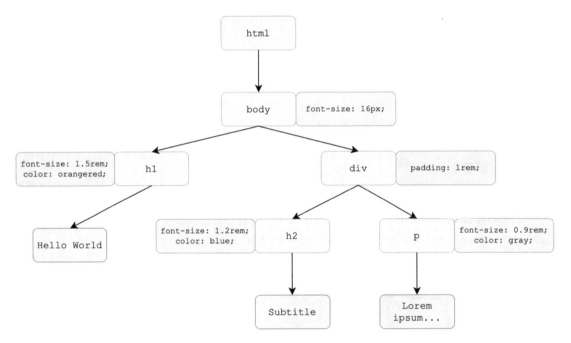

Figure 1-5. *The render tree*

Layout and paint

Once the browser has created the render tree, it can begin laying out the elements on the page. This stage of the process looks at styles such as width, height, position, margin, and padding, to determine each element's size and location on the page. At the layout stage, however, nothing is actually shown on screen yet.

Once layout is complete, the browser can begin painting by applying styles such as color and font to determine the actual pixels to draw on the screen. Some types of styles, like gradients, have a higher performance impact than a solid color or image.

Summary

In this chapter, we learned about

- The syntax and structure of CSS rules

- How conflicts are handled

- The three ways to use CSS in an HTML document – inline styles, style blocks, and external style sheets

- CSS preprocessors

- The critical rendering path – the DOM, CSSOM, and render tree

CHAPTER 2

CSS Selectors

One of the core concepts in CSS is that of selectors. A selector determines which element(s) a CSS rule applies to. There are several ways an element can be targeted with a selector, which we will cover in this chapter.

CSS selectors can target multiple elements on the page. That is, a single CSS rule can apply to multiple elements. An element or class selector can select multiple different elements that have that class or element name.

Similarly, a single HTML element can be affected by multiple CSS rules. An element will have the properties from all applicable CSS rules applied to it.

Basic selector types

The basic types of selectors are

- Universal
- Element
- ID
- Class
- Attribute

The universal selector

The universal selector, specified simply as an asterisk (*), matches all elements. This can be specified as a single selector, to select all elements in the document, or with combinators (discussed in the next section). Listing 2-1 shows an example usage of the universal selector.

© Joe Attardi 2020
J. Attardi, *Modern CSS*, https://doi.org/10.1007/978-1-4842-6294-8_2

Listing 2-1. Removing all margins with the universal selector

```
* {
  margin: 0;
}
```

The CSS rule in Listing 2-1 will apply a `margin` of `0` to all elements in the document.

Element selectors

An element selector targets an HTML element by its tag name. The syntax of the selector is simply the name of the element. Listing 2-2 shows an example usage of an element selector.

Listing 2-2. Applying a margin to all `div` elements

```
p {
  margin: 25px;
}
```

The CSS rule in Listing 2-2 will apply a margin of `25px` to all p elements in the document.

ID selectors

An HTML element can have an `id` attribute. As a general rule, there should only be one element with a given `id`. If there are multiple elements with the same `id`, most browsers will match the rule with all elements having that `id`. However, this should be avoided as it violates the HTML specification.

An ID selector is specified with the # character followed by the `id` value, as shown in Listing 2-3.

Listing 2-3. Applying padding to the element with an `id` of `header`

```
#header {
  padding: 25px;
}
```

The element with an id attribute whose value is header will receive 25px of padding. If there are other elements also having an id of header, they will receive 25px of padding in most browsers. Again, this should be avoided. If you need to apply a style to more than one element, you can use class selectors instead of ID selectors.

Class selectors

An HTML element can also have a class attribute. A class can be used to mark all elements of a related type.

While only a single element is intended to be targeted by an ID selector, any number of HTML elements can have the same class attribute. Similarly, a single HTML element can have any number of classes applied to it. Multiple classes are separated by a space in the value of the class attribute.

A class selector will match every element in the document with the given class. Class selectors are specified with a dot, followed by the name of the class, as shown in Listing 2-4.

Listing 2-4. Applying a color to all elements with the class nav-link

```
.nav-link {
  color: darkcyan;
}
```

The rule in Listing 2-4 will match every element in the document with a class of nav-link and give it a color of darkcyan.

Attribute selectors

HTML elements can also be selected by their attribute values or by the presence of an attribute. The attribute is specified inside square brackets, and the attribute selector can take several forms.

[name]

Selects all elements that have the given attribute, regardless of its value.

[name="value"]

Selects all elements that have the given attribute, whose value is the string value.

[name~="value"]

Selects all elements that have the given attribute, whose value contains the string `value` separated by whitespace. Listing 2-5 contains two HTML elements with slightly different `title` attributes.

Listing 2-5. Example HTML elements

```
<div title="Hello World">Hello World</div>
<div title="HelloWorld">HelloWorld</div>
```

If we wrote a CSS rule with the selector `[title~="World"]`, the first element would match but not the second. This is because in the second element, the word "World" in the title attribute is not surrounded by whitespace.

[name*="value"]

Selects all elements that have the given attribute, whose value contains the substring `value`. If we wrote another CSS rule, this time with the selector `[title*="World"]`, it would match both of the preceding elements.

[name^="value"]

Selects all elements that have the given attribute, whose value begins with `value`.

[name$="value"]

Selects all elements that have the given attribute, whose value ends with `value`.

Compound selectors

Any of the preceding selectors (with the exception of the universal selector) can be used alone or in conjunction with other selectors to make the selector more specific. This is best illustrated with some examples:

```
div.my-class
```

Matches all `div` elements with a class of `my-class`.

```
span.class-one.class-two
```

Matches all `span` elements with a class of *both* `class-one` and `class-two`.

```
a.nav-link[href*="example.com"]
```

Matches all `a` elements with a class of `nav-link` that have an `href` attribute that contains the string `example.com`.

Multiple independent selectors

A CSS rule can have multiple selectors separated by a comma. The rule will be applied to any element that is matched by any one of the given selectors.

```
.class-one, .class-two
```

Matches all elements with a class of `class-one` as well as all elements with a class of `class-two`.

Selector combinators

There's even more you can do with selectors. Combinators are used to select more specific elements. Combinators are used in conjunction with the basic selectors discussed earlier. For a given rule, multiple basic selectors can be used, joined by a combinator.

Descendant combinator

The descendant combinator matches an element that is a descendant of the element on the left-hand side. *Descendant* means that the element exists somewhere within the child hierarchy – it does not have to be a direct child.

The descendant combinator is specified with a space character:

```
.header div
```

Matches all div elements that are direct or indirect children of an element with a class of header. If any of these div elements have children that are also divs, those divs will also be matched by the selector.

Child combinator

The child combinator matches an element that is a *direct child* of the element on the left-hand side. It is specified with a > character:

```
.header > div
```

Matches all div elements that are direct children of an element with a class of header. If those divs have children that are also divs, those divs will *not* be matched by the selector.

General sibling combinator

The general sibling combinator matches an element that is a sibling, but not necessarily an *immediate* sibling, of the element on the left-hand side. It is specified with a ~ character. Consider the example in Listing 2-6.

Listing 2-6. Example HTML elements

```
<div>
  <div class="header"></div>
  <div class="body"></div>
  <div class="footer"></div>
</div>
```

The selector .header ~ div would match two div elements: the one with class body and the one with class footer. Note that it does not match the div with class header.

Adjacent sibling combinator

The adjacent sibling combinator is similar to the general sibling combinator, except it only matches elements that are an *immediate* sibling. It is specified with a + character.

Looking back at the HTML in Listing 2-6, the selector .header + div would only match the body element, because it is the adjacent sibling of the heading element.

Using multiple combinators

Just like basic selectors, combinators can be combined to form even more specific selectors. For example, this selector will match a button element that is an immediate sibling of a div element, which in turn is an immediate child of a div with the class header:

```
div.header > div + button
```

Pseudo-classes

Another tool in the CSS selector toolbox is the pseudo-class. A pseudo-class allows you to select elements based on some special state of the element, in addition to all the selectors previously discussed.

Pseudo-classes start with a colon and can be used alone or in conjunction with other selectors.

Some pseudo-classes let you select elements based on UI state, while others let you select elements based on their position in the document (with more precision than the combinators).

There are many pseudo-classes (you can find a complete list at `https://developer.mozilla.org/en-US/docs/Web/CSS/Pseudo-classes`), but here are some of the more commonly used ones.

UI state

These pseudo-classes are based on some UI state.

:active

Matches an element that is currently being activated. For buttons and links, this usually means the mouse button has been pressed but not yet released.

:checked

Matches a radio button, checkbox, or option inside a `select` element that is checked or selected.

:focus

Matches an element that currently has the focus. This is typically used for buttons, links, and text fields.

:hover

Matches an element that the mouse cursor is currently hovering over. This is typically used for buttons and links but can be applied to any type of element.

:valid, :invalid

Used with form elements using HTML5 validation. The :valid pseudo-class matches an element which is currently valid according to the validation rules, and :invalid matches an element which is not currently valid.

:visited

Matches a link whose URL has already been visited by the user. To protect a user's privacy, the browser limits what styling can be done on an element matched by this pseudo-class.

Document structure

These pseudo-classes are based on an element's position in the document.

:first-child, :last-child

Matches an element that is the first or last child of its parent. Consider the example unordered list in Listing 2-7.

Listing 2-7. A simple unordered list

```
<ul class="my-list">
  <li>Item one</li>
  <li>Item two</li>
</ul>
```

The selector `.my-list > li:first-child` will match the first list item only, and the selector `.my-list > li:last-child` will match the last list item only.

:nth-child(n)

This pseudo-class takes an argument. It matches an element that is the *n*th child of its parent. The index of the first child is 1. Referring back to Listing 2-7, we could also select the first item with the selector `.my-list > li:nth-child(1)`, or the second item with the selector `.my-list > li:nth-child(2)`.

The `:nth-child` pseudo-class can also select children at a given interval. For example, in a longer list, we could select every other list item with the selector `.my-list > li:nth-child(2n)`. Or we could select every four items with the selector `.my-list > li:nth-child(4n)`. We can even select all odd-numbered children with the selector `.my-list > li:nth-child(odd)` or even-numbered children with `.my-list > li:nth-child(even)`.

:nth-of-type(n)

Similar to `:nth-child`, except that it only considers children of the same type. For example, the selector `div:nth-of-type(2)` matches any `div` element that is the second `div` element among any group of children.

:root

Matches the root element of the document. This is usually the `html` element. This selector can be useful for several reasons, one of which is that it can be used to declare global variables (we will discuss CSS variables in Chapter 3).

Negating a selector

A selector can also include the `:not()` pseudo-class. `:not` accepts a selector as its argument and will match any element for which the selector does *not* match. For example, the selector `div:not(.fancy)` will match any `div` that does not have the `fancy` class.

Pseudo-elements

A pseudo-element lets you select only part of a matched element. Pseudo-elements are specified with a double colon (::) followed by the pseudo-element name.

We haven't discussed block vs. inline elements yet, but it should be noted that some pseudo-elements only apply to block-level elements.

::first-line

Matches the first line of a block element.

::first-letter

Applies the styles only to the first letter of the first line of an element.

::before, ::after

Two special pseudo-elements are ::before and ::after. These pseudo-elements don't select part of the element; rather, they actually create a new element as either the first child or the last child of the matched element, respectively. These pseudo-elements are typically used to decorate or add effects to an element.

Suppose we want to add an indicator next to all external links on our website. We can tag these external links using a class, say, external-link.

We can specify an external link as shown in Listing 2-8.

Listing 2-8. An external link

```
<a class="external-link"
   href="https://google.com">
  Google
</a>
```

Then we can add the indicator with the CSS rule in Listing 2-9. The content property defines what the text content of the pseudo-element should be.

Listing 2-9. Adding the external link indicator

```
.external-link::after {
  content: ' (external)';
  color: green;
}
```

Figure 2-1 shows the rendered HTML.

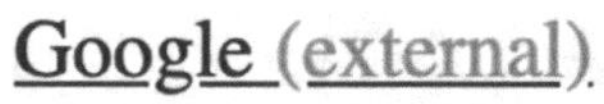

Google (external)

Figure 2-1. *The rendered link with an ::after pseudo-element*

The ::after pseudo-element added the content (external) and made it green.

Sometimes, you may want to use a ::before or ::after pseudo-element for decorative purposes. In this case, you must still provide a value for the content property or else the element will not be displayed. For decorative elements, this can be set to an empty string.

Specificity

An HTML element can have multiple CSS rules applied to it by matching different selectors. What happens if two or more of the rules applied to an element contain the same CSS property? How are such conflicts resolved? Listing 2-10 shows such a conflict.

Listing 2-10. Conflicting CSS rules

```
<style>
  .profile {
    background-color: green;
  }

  div {
    background-color: red;
    color: white;
  }
</style>

<div class="profile">My Profile</div>
```

We have a conflict. Our HTML element matches both selectors – it is indeed a `div` element, and it also has the `profile` class. Each rule specifies a different value for the `background-color` property. When the page is rendered, which background color will this `div` element have?

You might think that, since the element selector rule comes after the class selector rule, the element selector rule will win the conflict. After all, this is how conflicting CSS properties within a rule work. Figure 2-2 shows the output of this code.

Figure 2-2. *The rendered output*

As you can see, the class selector rule's background color was applied. This is because the class selector rule has a higher *specificity*. When there is a conflict of CSS properties across multiple rules, the rule with the most specific selector will be chosen. According to the rules of CSS, a class selector is more specific than an element selector.

Note that while the element has the background color from the class selector rule, it also has the color from the element selector rule. Specificity rules only matter for conflicting properties across multiple rules. Other properties in these multiple rules will still be applied.

Specificity rankings

The specificity rankings of CSS rules are as follows, from most specific to least specific:

1.   Inline styles in an element's `style` attribute

2.   ID selectors

3.   Class selectors, attribute selectors, and pseudo-classes

4.   Element selectors and pseudo-elements

Neither the universal selector nor combinators factor into specificity.

Calculating specificity

There is a general algorithm for calculating a CSS rule's specificity. To calculate the specificity of a CSS rule, imagine four boxes, one for each type of style rule in the given list, as shown in Figure 2-3. Initially, each box has a zero in it.

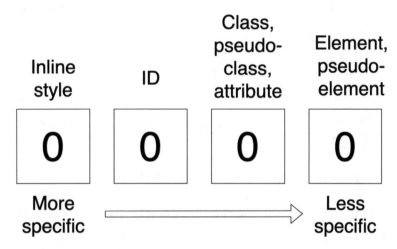

Figure 2-3. *Specificity calculator*

If the element has an inline style, add a 1 to the first box. In this case, the inline style automatically wins.

For each ID in the selector, add 1 to the value in the second box. For each class, pseudo-class, or attribute in the selector, add 1 to the value in the third box. Finally, for each element or pseudo-element in the selector, add 1 to the value in the last box.

Consider an example, the selector ul#primary-nav li.active. This would result in the specificity calculation shown in Figure 2-4.

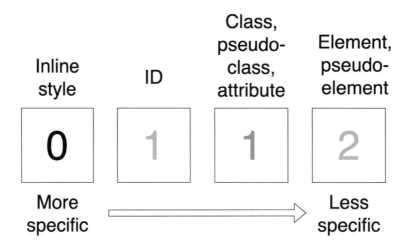

Figure 2-4. *Calculating the specificity of a selector*

Let's calculate the specificity of the two CSS selectors from Listing 2-10. Figure 2-5 shows the specificity values.

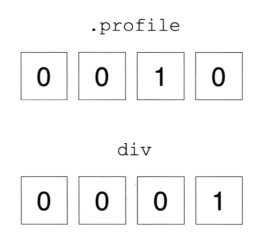

Figure 2-5. *Calculating the specificity values of the example selectors*

How do we interpret these specificity values? For most selectors, you can think of each number as the digit of a larger number and strip the leading zeros. The CSS specification states

> *Concatenating the four numbers a-b-c-d (in a number system with a large base) gives the specificity.*

This would give us values of 10 for the class selector and 1 for the element selector. Looking at it this way, it is clear that the class selector is more specific.

Figure 2-6 shows a comparison of two very similar selectors.

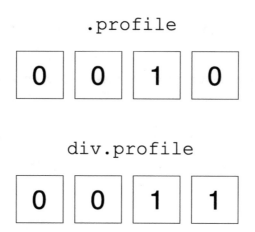

Figure 2-6. *Specificity calculation for two similar selectors*

These selectors are very similar, but the one containing both an element and a class selector (specificity 11) is more specific than the one containing a class selector alone (specificity 10).

Lastly, if multiple conflicting rules are calculated to have the same specificity, the rule that appears last will win.

The escape hatch: `!important`

Any CSS property can have the keyword `!important` after it inside of a rule. This keyword will cause that property to always win in a conflict, even if the rule that contains it has lower specificity than another conflicting rule.

However, this is generally considered a bad practice. It can make CSS issues harder to debug and can make your style sheets less maintainable. In most cases, it's better to determine the specificity of the rules you are trying to apply and use a more specific selector on the rule that you want to apply.

Summary

In this chapter, we learned all about CSS selector syntax and specificity rules. Some key takeaways are

- The most commonly used selectors are element, ID, class, and attribute selectors.

- Combinators can be used to create even more specific selectors.

- Multiple selectors can match an element.

- Conflicts are resolved by using the rule that is more specific.

- Specificity can be overridden by using `!important`, but this should be avoided.

CHAPTER 3

Basic CSS Concepts

Now that we've looked in detail at how to select elements, let's start to explore how to style them. The next step is to look at some of the basic concepts in CSS.

The box model

Every element in CSS is treated like a rectangular box. This is sometimes referred to as the box model. The box is made up of four parts. Starting from the outside and moving toward the center, these are the margin, border, padding, and content.

The margin is the space between an element's border and its surrounding elements. It is specified with the `margin` property.

The border is an outline around the box. Borders can be styled with a thickness, style, and color. It is specified with several properties: `border-style`, `border-width`, `border-color`, and `border`.

The padding is the space between the element's border and the content itself. It is specified with the `padding` property.

Figure 3-1 shows the different parts of the CSS box model.

© Joe Attardi 2020
J. Attardi, *Modern CSS*, https://doi.org/10.1007/978-1-4842-6294-8_3

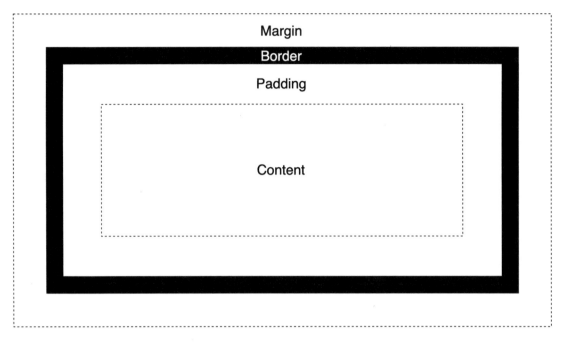

Figure 3-1. *The CSS box model*

By default, most elements have no padding, border, or margin. There are some exceptions, like button elements. Listing 3-1 shows two div elements with some color to differentiate them but no other styling applied.

Listing 3-1. Two simple `div` elements

```
<style>
  #div1 {
    background-color: red;
  }

  #div2 {
    background-color: green;
  }

  div {
    color: white;
  }
</style>
```

```
<div id="div1">Hello world!</div>
<div id="div2">Hello world!</div>
```

Figure 3-2 shows the rendered result of these two elements.

Figure 3-2. *The rendered result*

Notice how the elements run up against one another and generally look cramped. By adding padding, border, and margin to these elements, we can make it easier to read. Listing 3-2 adds these properties.

Listing 3-2. Applying padding, border, and margin

```
<style>
  #div1 {
    background-color: red;
  }

  #div2 {
    background-color: green;
  }

  div {
    color: white;
    padding: 1rem;
    margin: 1rem;
    border: 2px solid black;
  }
</style>

<div id="div1">Hello world!</div>
<div id="div2">Hello world!</div>
```

Figure 3-3 shows the elements with their new styling.

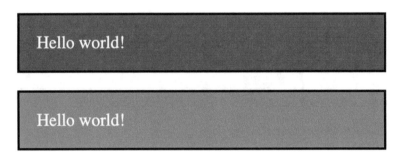

Figure 3-3. *The same two elements with padding, border, and margin applied*

Box sizing

The size of an element is specified with the width and height properties. How exactly this is interpreted, however, depends on the value of the box-sizing property. This property supports two values, content-box and border-box.

content-box

This is the default. With content-box, the width and height properties are treated as the width and height of the content area of the box only. The actual width and height taken up by the element's box is the sum of the specified width and height (the content box), the padding on each side, and the border width on each side.

Consider the example rule in Listing 3-3.

Listing 3-3. A simple CSS rule

```
.box {
  width: 100px;
  height: 100px;
  padding: 10px;
  border: 2px solid red;
}
```

The actual width and height taken up by the rendered box will be 100px + 10px + 10px + 2px + 2px = 124 pixels, as visualized in Figure 3-4.

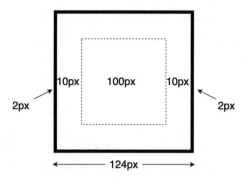

Figure 3-4. *The full rendered size of the element using* content-box

border-box

With border-box, the values of the width and height properties are treated as the size of the content box plus the padding and border width. Looking back at the example in Listing 3-3, and setting box-sizing to border-box, the total width and height of the rendered element is 100 pixels. To compensate for the extra 24 pixels taken up by the padding and border width, the size of the content box will shrink to 76 pixels, as visualized in Figure 3-5.

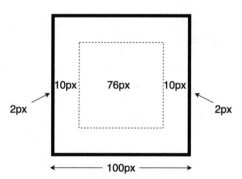

Figure 3-5. *The full rendered size of the element using* border-box

Block and inline elements

There are two types of HTML elements: block and inline (or a combination of the two, inline-block). Both block and inline elements follow the box model but are different in some important ways.

Some HTML elements are block elements (e.g., div) and some are inline elements (e.g., span). An element's type can be changed by setting the display property to block, inline, or inline-block.

Block elements

A block element always appears on its own line and takes up the full width of its containing element, unless an explicit width is set with the width property. The height of a block element, by default, is just enough to fit the height of its content, but this height can also explicitly be set with the height property.

The example in Listing 3-4 contains some div elements, which are block elements.

Listing 3-4. Some div elements

```
<style>
  .container {
    width: 350px;
    border: 2px solid black;
  }

  .box1 {
    background-color: skyblue;
  }

  .box2 {
    background-color: lime;
  }
</style>

<div class="container">
  <div class="box1">Hello</div>
  <div class="box2">World</div>
</div>
```

The rendered result is shown in Figure 3-6.

Figure 3-6. *The* div *elements rendered as block elements*

The outer container element has an explicit width of 350px set, so it will be 350 pixels wide (technically, 354 pixels, since it is using content-box sizing).

The inner elements have no explicit width set, so they take up the full width of the container element. They also have no explicit height set, so they only take up enough vertical space to fit the text content.

Inline elements

Unlike block elements, an inline element is rendered inside the normal flow of text. They only take up enough width and height as necessary to contain their content. Setting the width or height properties of an inline element will have no effect. Listing 3-5 has an example of an inline element.

Listing 3-5. An inline span element

```
<style>
  .highlight {
    background-color: yellow;
  }
</style>
Hello <span class="highlight">world</span>, I am demonstrating an inline
element.
```

Figure 3-7 shows the rendered result.

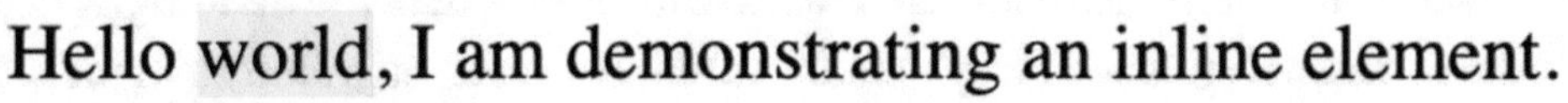

Hello world, I am demonstrating an inline element.

Figure 3-7. *The rendered inline element*

The span is an inline element, so its width and height are only enough to fit its content. As you can see, it does not appear on its own line. If we were to give the span an explicit width or height, it would be ignored.

There are some other differences between block and inline elements as well. When setting padding on the left and right of an inline element, it behaves as expected. The padding is applied, and the element takes up extra space. Listing 3-6 has an example that illustrates this.

Listing 3-6. Horizontal padding on an inline element

```
<style>
  .container {
    width: 300px;
  }

  .highlight {
    background-color: yellow;
    padding-left: 50px;
    padding-right: 50px;
  }
</style>

<div class="container">
  Hello <span class="highlight">world</span>, I am demonstrating an inline
element.
</div>
```

The result is shown in Figure 3-8.

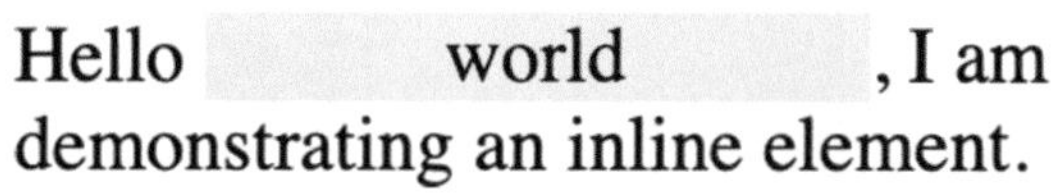

Hello   world   , I am demonstrating an inline element.

Figure 3-8. *The rendered result*

As expected, the element's width increases to accommodate the padding, and the surrounding content is pushed away to make room. However, an inline element behaves differently when setting top and bottom padding. Consider Listing 3-7.

Listing 3-7. Adding vertical padding to an inline element

```
<style>
  .container {
    width: 300px;
  }

  .highlight {
    background-color: yellow;
    padding-left: 50px;
    padding-right: 50px;
    padding-top: 50px;
    padding-bottom: 50px;
  }
</style>

<div class="container">
  Hello <span class="highlight">world</span>, I am demonstrating an inline
element.
</div>
```

The result, shown in Figure 3-9, may surprise you.

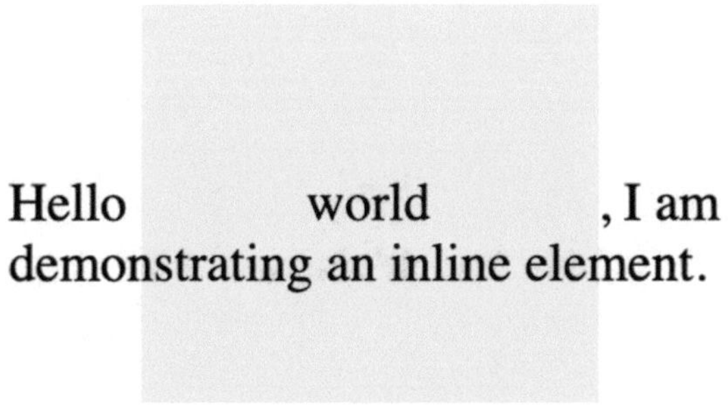

Hello   world   , I am
demonstrating an inline element.

Figure 3-9. *The odd behavior of vertical padding on an inline element*

The padding was applied to the element, but no extra vertical space was made to accommodate the top and bottom padding. The background color of the span element bleeds into the adjacent content.

Inline elements behave similarly when it comes to margins – extra space is made for the horizontal margins but not the vertical ones.

41

Inline-block elements

The third element type is a combination of the first two. An inline-block element flows with the text like an inline element, but the width and height properties are respected, as are the vertical padding and margin.

Listing 3-8 takes the example from Listing 3-5 and makes the element an inline-block element and gives it an explicit width.

Listing 3-8. Using an inline-block element

```
<style>
  .container {
    width: 300px;
  }

  .highlight {
    background-color: yellow;
    display: inline-block;
    width: 100px;
    padding-left: 50px;
    padding-right: 50px;
    padding-top: 50px;
    padding-bottom: 50px;
  }
</style>

<div class="container">
  Hello <span class="highlight">world</span>, I am demonstrating an inline-
  block element.
</div>
```

The result is shown in Figure 3-10.

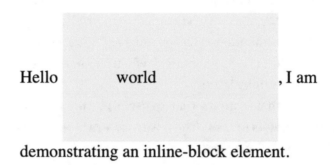

Hello   world   , I am

demonstrating an inline-block element.

Figure 3-10. *The rendered inline-block element*

The span element does not break onto a new line – it flows with the text like an inline element. However, its width and height properties are respected, as is the vertical padding. Extra space is made to account for the padding – it doesn't bleed over into the surrounding content like with an inline element.

Units

To give an element a padding of 10 pixels, we would specify a value of 10px for the padding property. In this expression, we say that px is a unit. CSS units are equivalent to different units of measurement. In the physical world, measurements have units such as inches, feet, or meters. Similarly, CSS has units such as px, em, and rem. We will go over some of these in this section.

px

We've already seen the px unit in several examples. In the past, we could have said that this corresponds to physical pixels on the screen. However, in the modern age of ultrahigh-resolution displays, this is no longer exactly accurate. A CSS pixel does not necessarily have a one-to-one correspondence to a physical device pixel. On a very high-resolution 4K display, 1 pixel is so tiny that it would be hard to see with the naked eye. If CSS used device pixels, then a 1-pixel border would barely be visible to the user.

Instead, a so-called logical pixel corresponds to a certain number of physical device pixels. A 1px border looks roughly equivalent on a 4K display as it does on a lower resolution display, but it may use more physical device pixels.

It is generally not recommended to use px units in CSS. The main reason is that these pixel-based dimensions don't always scale well when a user adjusts the browser zoom level. This can be an accessibility issue.

There is one property that is appropriate to use pixels for – the page's base font size. In most browsers, this defaults to 16px. The base font size is set by applying the font-size property to the root html element.

It's also appropriate to use pixels in media queries, which we will cover in Chapter 11.

em

The em unit is a relative unit. It is relative to the font size of the element. Listing 3-9 shows a rule using the em unit for padding.

Listing 3-9. Using the em unit

```
.header {
  font-size: 24px;
  padding: 0.5em;
}
```

The header element has a font size of 24px. The padding is specified as 0.5em, or half of the element's font size. Therefore, the padding applied to this element will be 12px.

Listing 3-10 shows another example of using the em unit.

Listing 3-10. Specifying the font size in em units

```
.header {
  font-size: 24px;
  padding: 0.5em;
}

.header li {
  font-size: 0.75em;
}
```

```
.header li a {
  font-size: 0.5em;
}
```

Because font size is inherited, the li elements inside the header also start out with a font size of 24px. Then in the li element's CSS rule, we set the font size to 0.75em. This is relative to the element's current font size of 24px, so the actual font size of the li element would be 24px * 0.75 = 18px. Finally, the a elements inside the li elements have a font-size of 0.5em, which is relative to the li element's font size of 18px, so its font size would be 18px * 0.5 = 9px.

Due to this cascading effect, sometimes using em units for nested elements can cause unintended effects to properties such as font size, padding, and margin.

rem

The rem unit is also a relative unit. It stands for "root em" and is relative to the page's base font size. For example, if the base font size is 16px (remember that this usually doesn't correspond to physical pixels), a size of 1rem is equal to 16px. 1.5rem would be 16px * 1.5 = 24px.

rem units are a good choice, especially for layout properties, since the size of 1rem remains constant throughout the document (unlike the em unit). If the browser is zoomed, everything resizes nicely because it's all proportional to the base font size.

Because rem units are proportional to the base font size, there is no cascading effect like there is with em units.

Viewport units: vw and vh

The *viewport* is the area of the page that is currently visible in your web browser. CSS also has units that are relative to the viewport size: vw (viewport width) and vh (viewport height). Each of these units are 1% of the viewport size in that direction, that is, 1vw is 1% of the viewport width and 1vh is 1% of the viewport height.

If the viewport is resized, then any elements using vw units will have their sizes adjusted accordingly. Because vw and vh are relative to the viewport size, they are a good choice when using responsive design techniques.

There are also two related units, vmin and vmax. vmin is defined as whichever is smaller – the viewport width or the viewport height – and vmax is the larger of the two.

45

Percentage: %

The % unit is relative to the size of another value. What exactly this is relative to depends on the CSS property. For example, for the font-size property, the % unit is defined as a percentage of the parent element's font size. However, for the padding property, % is defined as a percentage of the element's width.

Like the viewport units, the percentage unit is very useful for responsive design, as we will see in Chapter 11.

No units

Some property values take no units at all but rather just a number. For example, the opacity property expects a number between 0 and 1. Another example of this is some flexbox properties such as flex-grow and flex-shrink, which expect integer numbers without units.

Other units

We have seen the most commonly used CSS units, but there are others as well. There are absolute units such as cm (centimeters), mm (millimeters), in (inches), and pt (points). These units are sometimes used for print style sheets but are rarely seen in screen style sheets.

There are also some experimental units that do not yet have wide browser support. For example, the lh unit is relative to the element's line height, but this unit is currently not supported on any browsers.

Functions

CSS includes some helpful built-in functions.

calc

The calc function lets you combine the different units we saw earlier to calculate an exact amount. It can be used anywhere a value is expected. The real power of the calc function is that you can have mixed units in the calculation.

For example, suppose you want the height of an element to be 10 pixels short of `1.5rem`. This can easily be accomplished with the `calc` function: `calc(1.5rem - 10px)`. This is likely easier than doing the size calculations yourself to specify an exact pixel value.

Another very useful feature of the `calc` function is that it also works with CSS custom properties, or variables. We will look at variables in Chapter 6, but Listing 3-11 has an example.

Listing 3-11. Using CSS variables with the `calc` function

```
:root {
  --spacing: 0.5rem
}

.container {
  padding: calc(var(--spacing) * 2);
}
```

In this example, we establish a standard unit of spacing for the document as a variable and can reference that later in the call to the `calc` function. You might also notice the `var` function, which as we will see later is used to reference variables.

There are several other functions, which we will cover in the relevant sections. For example, there are some functions for defining colors, which we will explore in the next section.

Colors

One of the most common things done with CSS is to change colors. This can include background color, text color, and border color. There are a multitude of colors, and they can be expressed in multiple ways.

Predefined colors

CSS has many predefined color values. So far, all of the examples in the book have used these predefined color values. They range from basics like `red` and `green` to other shades like `tomato`, `orangered`, and `skyblue`. A full list of these colors can be found at `https://developer.mozilla.org/en-US/docs/Web/CSS/color_value`.

RGB colors

One of the ways to define a color is by the values of the color's red, green, and blue components. Any color can be expressed as a combination of RGB values. Each value of red, green, and blue is expressed as a number between 0 and 255.

One way that an RGB color can be specified is as a hexadecimal value. The red, green, and blue values are each converted to two hexadecimal digits. These digits are used in RGB order, preceded by a pound sign (#). The hex values can be specified with uppercase or lowercase letters. Table 3-1 shows a few examples of RGB hex notation.

Table 3-1. *Example colors and their hex values*

Color	Hex code
Black	#000000
White	#FFFFFF
Red	#FF0000
Green	#00FF00
Blue	#0000FF

The other way to specify an RGB color is by using the rgb function. Instead of hexadecimal digits, the red, green, and blue components of the color are specified as base-10 numbers between 0 and 255 or a percentage between 0% and 100%. Table 3-2 shows the usage of the rgb function.

Table 3-2. *Example colors using the rgb function*

Color	RGB notation
Black	rgb(0, 0, 0)
White	rgb(255, 255, 255)
Red	rgb(255, 0, 0)
Green	rgb(0, 255, 0)
Blue	rgb(0, 0, 255)

Alpha value

RGB colors can also specify an alpha value, which determines the opacity of the color. The alpha is a value between 0 (fully transparent) and 1 (fully opaque) or a percentage between 0% and 100%. To specify an alpha value, the rgba function is used. For example, for pure red with 50% opacity, the color would be defined as rgba(255, 0, 0, 0.5).

HSL colors

A color can also be expressed as a combination of hue, saturation, and lightness values. Hue is specified as a degree of an angle on the color wheel (from 0 to 360 degrees). 0 degrees is red, 120 degrees is green, and 240 degrees is blue.

Saturation is a percentage value of how much color is applied. 0% saturation is a shade of gray, and 100% saturation is the full color from the color wheel.

Finally, lightness is also a percentage value. 0% lightness is pure black, and 100% is pure white.

An HSL color is specified using the hsl function. For the color with a hue of 120 degrees, a saturation of 50% and a lightness of 50% would be specified as hsl(120, 50%, 50%).

Like RGB colors, HSL colors can also have an alpha value, specified using the hsla function. As described earlier, the alpha value can be a number between 0 and 1 or a percentage between 0% and 100%. For the color in the previous example to have 75% opacity, it would be specified as hsla(120, 50%, 50%, 0.75).

Transparent

Anywhere a color is expected, the transparent keyword can be used. This will apply no color. This can be useful when an element is positioned on top of another element, and you want the element underneath to show through. The background color of most elements defaults to transparent.

Newer color syntax

The usage of the rgb/rgba and hsl/hsla functions as previously described has been the standard for a long time. There is a newer syntax for these functions that are slightly different. This newer format is completely optional, and in fact, if you have to support older browsers, you won't want to use it.

The new syntax makes a few changes:

- There are no commas between the numbers.

- If an alpha value is specified, it is separated from the three color values with a slash character:

  - Because of this, the rgba and hsla functions are no longer necessary. The alpha value can be specified with a slash in the base rgb and hsl functions.

- The alpha value can also be specified on a hex color, for example, #FF00007F for pure red with 50% alpha.

Table 3-3 shows some comparisons between the old and new syntax.

Table 3-3. *Comparison of old and new color syntax*

Old syntax	Equivalent new syntax
rgb(0, 0, 0)	rgb(0 0 0)
rgba(255, 0, 0, 0.5)	rgb(255 0 0 / 0.5)
hsl(120, 50%, 50%)	hsl(120 50% 50%)
hsla(120, 50%, 50%, 0.75)	hsl(120 50% 50% / 0.75)

Compatibility note   This new color syntax is not supported in Internet Explorer.

Overflow

As discussed earlier, every HTML element is a rectangular box. Normally, the size of an element expands to fit its content, as we have seen in some earlier examples. However, what happens when an explicit height is set and the content does not fit inside the element's dimensions? This is a condition known as *overflow*. Listing 3-12 contains an example showing text overflowing its container.

Listing 3-12. Demonstrating overflow of an element's content

```
<style>
  .container {
    background-color: skyblue;
    height: 2rem;
    width: 10rem;
  }
</style>

<div class="container">
  This is some really long text that will overflow the container.
</div>
```

The overflow can be seen in Figure 3-11.

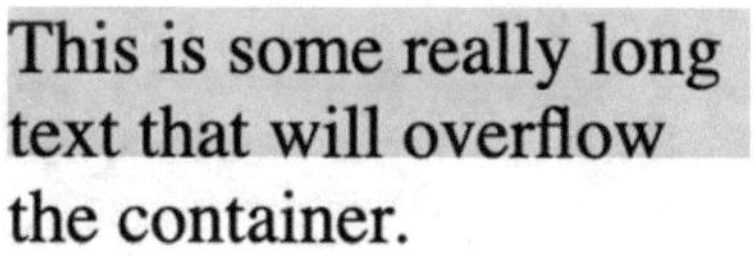

This is some really long
text that will overflow
the container.

Figure 3-11. *Text overflowing the container*

We can clearly see that the text content is too long to fit in a 2rem by 10rem container, so the content overflows the container element. Note that the content only overflows vertically. This is because the default behavior is to wrap the text to the next line when it doesn't fit on one line. This ensures it does not overflow horizontally, but because an explicit height is set, the container will not grow to fit its content.

If we insert a fixed-width element inside the container, as shown in Listing 3-13, the content will overflow both horizontally and vertically. We will add some padding to the container as well, to make the overflow more apparent.

Listing 3-13. Adding a fixed-width element inside the container

```
<style>
  .container {
    background-color: skyblue;
    height: 2rem;
    width: 10rem;
```

```
    padding: 1rem;
  }

  .container .banner {
    background-color: #999999;
    width: 15rem;
  }
</style>

<div class="container">
  <div class="banner">This is a banner</div>
  This is some really long text that will overflow the container.
</div>
```

Figure 3-12 shows that there is now horizontal as well as vertical overflow.

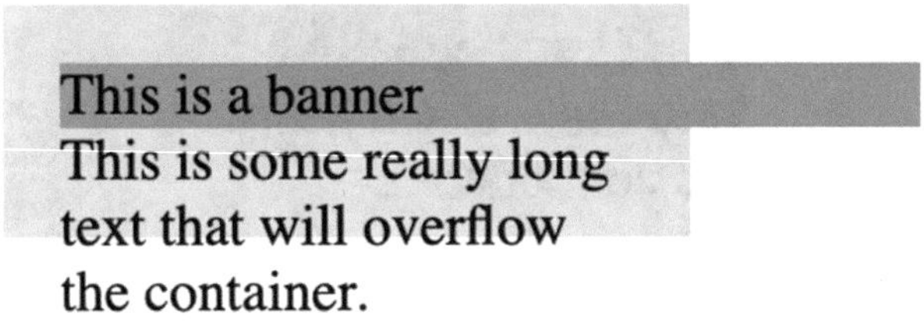

This is a banner
This is some really long
text that will overflow
the container.

Figure 3-12. *Horizontal and vertical overflow*

As we now know, the content inside a block element will wrap to a new line when it doesn't fit horizontally. We can change this behavior with the white-space property. If we set this property to nowrap in the first example from Listing 3-12, as shown in Listing 3-14, this will also cause horizontal overflow.

Listing 3-14. Setting white-space to nowrap

```
<style>
  .container {
    background-color: skyblue;
    height: 2rem;
    width: 10rem;
    white-space: nowrap;
  }
</style>
```

```
<div class="container">
  This is some really long text that will overflow the container.
</div>
```

As Figure 3-13 shows, this has caused horizontal overflow.

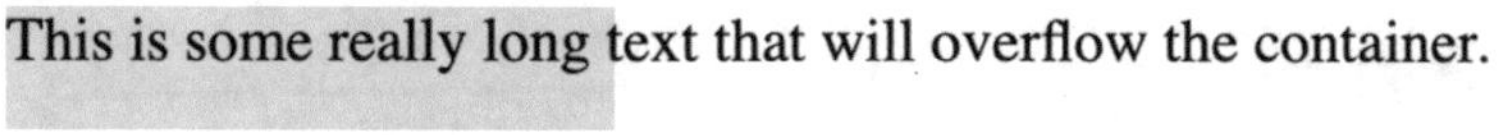

This is some really long text that will overflow the container.

Figure 3-13. *Horizontal overflow of the container's text content*

Handling overflow

We have some control over how overflow is handled with the overflow property. This property handles both horizontal and vertical overflow together. They can also be handled independently with the overflow-x and overflow-y properties. The default value is visible, which results in what we saw in the previous examples. There are a few other options available.

hidden

When the overflow property is set to hidden, the overflowing content is simply not displayed. It is clipped by the bounds of the containing element, as shown in Figure 3-14.

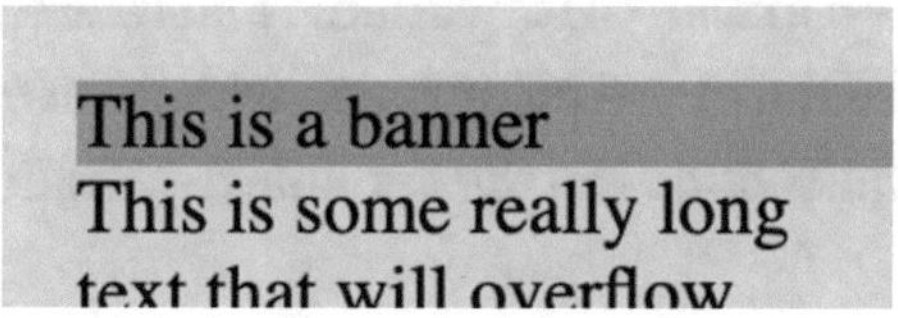

This is a banner
This is some really long
text that will overflow

Figure 3-14. *The overflowing content is clipped with overflow: hidden*

scroll

When the overflow property is set to scroll, the overflowing content is initially not visible. However, there are scrollbars provided so that the user can scroll and view the overflowing content. The scrollbars are always provided, even if the content does not overflow.

auto

This behaves similarly to scroll. The difference is that when overflow is set to auto, the scrollbars are only provided if the content actually overflows.

CSS variables

Variables are a common feature in all programming languages. A variable is a way to store a piece of data, under a descriptive name, and that value can be referenced later by the variable name.

Variables have been available for many years with CSS preprocessing tools like Sass and Less. CSS variables, officially called *CSS custom properties*, were introduced later. Support for CSS variables was not great until more recently. They are now supported in all modern browsers.

Compatibility note   CSS variables are not supported in Internet Explorer.

Why would we want to use variables in CSS? Suppose you're designing a website for a company. You use their brand color, #3FA2D9, in many places throughout your CSS. Later, the site is going through a rebranding, and the brand color is changing. You now have to change the brand color in every place you used #3FA2D9.

Instead, you can define a brand-color variable and reference that variable everywhere you need to use the brand color. Later, when that color changes, you simply need to change the color value once – in the variable declaration.

Using variables

CSS variables are declared with two dashes followed by the variable name, such as

```
--brand-color: #3FA2D9;
```

To reference a variable's value later, you need to pass the variable name to the var function:

```
background-color: var(--brand-color);
```

The var function also takes an optional second argument, which is a fallback value to use in case the variable isn't defined:

```
background-color: var(--brand-color, #3FA2D9);
```

Variable inheritance

A variable can be declared on any element or pseudo-element. Variables then cascade down to descendant elements, as demonstrated in Listing 3-15. The result is shown in Figure 3-15.

Listing 3-15. Inheriting a parent's variable

```
<style>
  .container {
    --heading-color: blue;
    font-family: Arial, sans-serif;
  }

  .container h1 {
    color: var(--heading-color);
  }
</style>

<div class="container">
  <h1>Welcome</h1>
</div>
```

Welcome

Figure 3-15. *The rendered result*

To make a variable apply to the entire document (a so-called global variable), you can set it using the special :root selector, as shown in Listing 3-16.

Listing 3-16. A global variable

```
<style>
  :root {
    --text-color: red;
  }

  .container {
    color: var(--text-color);
    font-family: Arial, sans-serif;
  }
</style>

<div class="container">Hello World!</div>
```

Variables can also reference other variables, as shown in Listing 3-17. The result is shown in Figure 3-16.

Listing 3-17. Referencing variables inside other variables

```
<style>
  :root {
    --primary-border-color: red;
    --primary-border-style: solid;
    --primary-border-width: 3px;
    --primary-border:
      var(--primary-border-width)
      var(--primary-border-style)
      var(--primary-border-color);
  }

  .container {
    border: var(--primary-border);
    width: 10rem;
  }
</style>

<div class="container">Hello World!</div>
```

Hello World!

Figure 3-16. *The rendered result*

Using variables in CSS calculations

Finally, you can even reference variables in the calc function. Consider the example in
Listing 3-18. We have a container with six rows. We want the container to be tall enough
to show three visible rows, and the rest should overflow and be accessed via scroll. The
result is shown in Figure 3-17.

Listing 3-18. Using variables for layout

```
<style>
  :root {
    --row-height: 1.5rem;
    --visible-rows: 3;
  }

  .container {
    border: 1px solid red;
    height: calc(var(--row-height) * var(--visible-rows));
    overflow: auto;
    width: 10rem;
  }

  .row {
    line-height: var(--row-height);
  }
</style>

<div class="container">
  <div class="row">Row one</div>
  <div class="row">Row two</div>
  <div class="row">Row three</div>
  <div class="row">Row four</div>
```

```
  <div class="row">Row five</div>
  <div class="row">Row six</div>
</div>
```

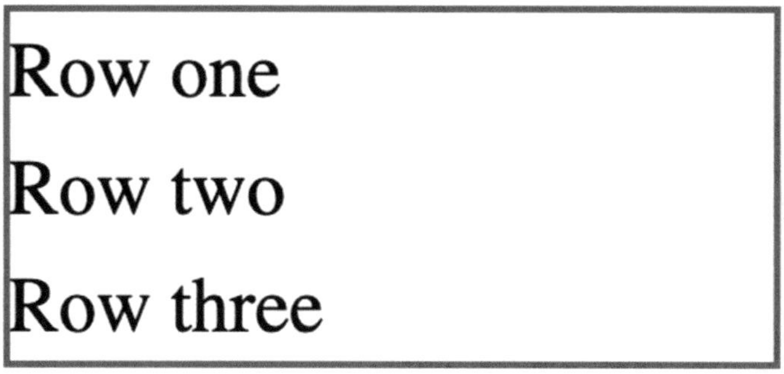

```
Row one

Row two

Row three
```

Figure 3-17. *Three visible rows*

We set two variables: an explicit row height of 1.5rem and a visible row count of 3. The container should be as high as three rows, so in the .container rule, we use calc to multiply the --row-height variable by the --visible-rows variable, which will yield exactly the correct height.

We also apply overflow: auto, which as we saw earlier hides the overflow and makes it scrollable.

Summary

In this chapter, we learned about some of the basic concepts of CSS. Some key takeaways are

- All elements are represented by a rectangular box with content, padding, border, and margin.

- There are three main types of elements: block, inline, and inline-block.

- There are many different units for CSS values:

  - px should be avoided except when setting the document's base font size.

  - em is relative to the element's font size.

- rem is relative to the document's base font size.

- vw, vh, vmin, and vmax are relative to the viewport size.

- The calc function is used to compute CSS values by performing calculations with multiple values, potentially with different units.

- Colors can be defined in several ways.

  - Named colors: red, blue, and orangered

  - Hexadecimal RGB: #FF0000

  - rgb function: rgb(255, 0, 0)

  - hsl function: hsl(90, 50%, 25%)

- If an element's content cannot fit inside of it, the content will overflow.

- Overflow handling can be changed with the overflow, overflow-x, and overflow-y properties.

- A variable is declared with two leading slashes: --var-name.

- A variable is referenced with the var function: var(--var-name).

- Variable values are inherited by descendant elements.

CHAPTER 4

Basic Styling

By now, you have a solid grasp of the main underlying concepts of CSS. Now it's time to dive in and start learning some CSS properties and styling techniques. We'll start with the basics in this chapter.

Property values

First, a few notes on CSS property values.

Global keywords

Most CSS properties support several *global keywords* as their values:

- `initial`: Uses the initial value set by the browser's built-in style sheet.

- `inherit`: Takes the value used by the element's parent.

- `unset`: If the property naturally inherits from its parent, such as `font-size`, it is set to the inherited value. Otherwise, it is set to the initial value from the browser's style sheet.

Shorthand and multiple values

We've seen how many CSS properties, such as `border-width`, `padding`, and `margin`, can take a single value. These are known as *shorthand properties*. For these properties, the single value given will be used for the top, bottom, left, and right.

Each shorthand property has four equivalent properties for each side of the element. For example, for the `padding` shorthand element, there are also `padding-top`, `padding-bottom`, `padding-left`, and `padding-right` properties.

© Joe Attardi 2020
J. Attardi, *Modern CSS*, https://doi.org/10.1007/978-1-4842-6294-8_4

If you want to specify different values for different sides of the element, you can still use the shorthand property – just give it multiple values.

If one value is given, as we've seen, it applies to all four sides of the element. Listing 4-1 shows an example of this using the border-width property.

Listing 4-1. A single value for the border-width property

```
<style>
  .container {
    border-color: red;
    border-style: solid;
    border-width: 1px;
  }
</style>

<div class="container">Hello world!</div>
```

You can see in Figure 4-1 that all four borders have the same width.

Hello world!

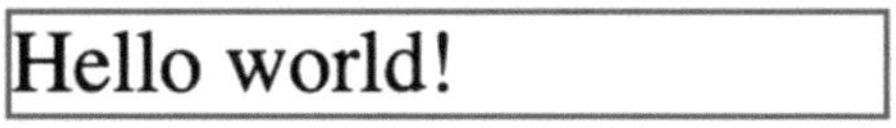

Figure 4-1. *All four borders have the same width*

If two values are specified, the first applies to the top and bottom, and the second applies to the left and right. An example of this is shown in Listing 4-2.

Listing 4-2. Two values for the border-width property

```
<style>
  .container {
    border-color: red;
    border-style: solid;
    border-width: 1px 5px;
  }
</style>

<div class="container">Hello world!</div>
```

Note the different border widths in Figure 4-2 on the top and bottom compared to the left and right.

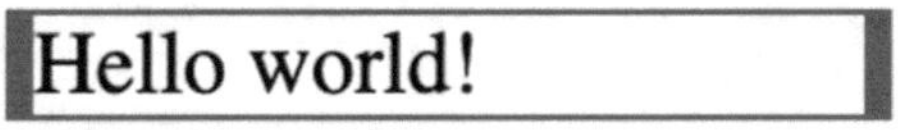

Figure 4-2. *The rendered result*

If three values are specified, the first applies to the top, the second applies to the left and right, and the third applies to the bottom. Listing 4-3 has an example of this, and the result is shown in Figure 4-3.

Listing 4-3. Three values for the border-width property

```
<style>
  .container {
    border-color: red;
    border-style: solid;
    border-width: 1px 5px 10px;
  }
</style>

<div class="container">Hello world!</div>
```

Figure 4-3. *The rendered result*

Finally, if four values are specified, they are applied in clockwise order, starting at the top.

Listing 4-4. Four values for the border-width property

```
<style>
  .container {
    border-color: red;
    border-style: solid;
    border-width: 1px 5px 10px 20px;
  }
</style>

<div class="container">Hello world!</div>
```

Figure 4-4. *All borders have different widths*

Borders

For most elements, the border is invisible by default. CSS has several properties for styling a border.

border-color

The border-color property, as its name implies, sets the color of the border.

border-width

The border-width property determines how thick the border is. The value of border-width can be a value like 3px. There are also some predefined values: thin, medium, and thick.

border-style

The border-style property determines the visual appearance of the border. In addition to none (the default), there are several available border styles, as shown in Figure 4-5.

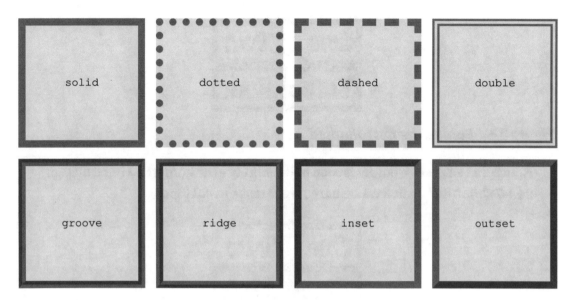

Figure 4-5. *The different border styles*

border

The three preceding properties can be combined into a single property with the border shorthand property, as shown in Listing 4-5. The properties can be specified in any order.

Listing 4-5. The border shorthand property

```
.container {
  border: 5px solid red;
}
```

border-collapse

The border-collapse property only applies to table elements. It controls how borders are preserved or collapsed between adjoining table cells. The default value is separate. With this default behavior, a table's borders are not combined. Consider the table in Figure 4-6, where each cell has a different-colored border.

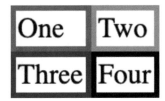

Figure 4-6. *Borders are not collapsed*

Notice that each cell's border is seen in its entirety – the borders do not collapse. Figure 4-7 shows the result if we set `border-collapse` to `collapse`.

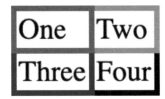

Figure 4-7. *Borders are now collapsed*

Any cell borders adjacent to another border have been collapsed into a single border.

border-radius

By default, blocks have 90-degree rectangular corners. That isn't always the most aesthetically pleasing design, though. To address this, CSS gives us the `border-radius` property. This property gives us rounded corners. The corners can be circular or elliptical. A simple example is shown in Listing 4-6.

Listing 4-6. Setting a border radius

```
<style>
  .rounded-corners {
    background-color: red;
    border-radius: 10px;
    height: 5rem;
    width: 5rem;
  }
</style>

<div class="rounded-corners"></div>
```

This creates rounded corners with a radius of 10px, as shown in Figure 4-8.

Figure 4-8. *A box with rounded corners*

What does it mean for the corner to have a radius of 10px? Imagine a circle drawn over each of the corners. That circle's radius is 10px. This visualization is shown in Figure 4-9.

Figure 4-9. *The meaning of border radius*

The border-radius can be elliptical as well as circular. Each of the two radii of the ellipse is specified, separated by a slash, as shown in Listing 4-7.

Listing 4-7. Using an elliptical border-radius

```
<style>
  .rounded-corners {
    background-color: red;
    border-radius: 20px / 10px;
```

```
    height: 5rem;
    width: 5rem;
  }
</style>

<div class="rounded-corners"></div>
```

Figure 4-10 shows the resulting corners.

Figure 4-10.   *The box with elliptical border radius*

Similar to the circular radius, the elliptical radius effect is applied with an ellipse in each corner. The horizontal radius is given first, followed by the vertical. This is illustrated in Figure 4-11.

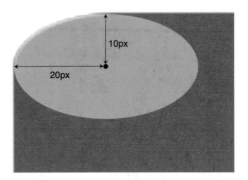

Figure 4-11.   *Explanation of the elliptical border radius*

You can also specify a different border-radius for each corner, as shown in Listing 4-8, creating some interesting shapes. Note that when you specify border-radius in this way, an elliptical border-radius does not have a slash separating the horizontal and vertical radius. The result is shown in Figure 4-12.

Listing 4-8. Specifying different border radius properties

```
<style>
  .rounded-corners {
    background-color: red;
    border-bottom-right-radius: 10px 20px;
    border-bottom-left-radius: 5px;
    border-top-left-radius: 20px 10px;
    border-top-right-radius: 50%;
    height: 5rem;
    width: 5rem;
  }
</style>

<div class="rounded-corners"></div>
```

Figure 4-12. *The resulting shape*

Box shadows

Elements can also have a shadow. This is controlled by the box-shadow property. A box shadow has a color, and its dimensions can be specified with up to four values, which are

- X offset

- Y offset

- Blur radius: How far out the shadow is blurred

- Spread radius: How far the shadow extends beyond the element's dimensions

At a minimum, the X and Y offsets must be given. By default, the blur and spread radius are zero. Listing 4-9 has a straightforward example. The result is shown in Figure 4-13.

Listing 4-9. A simple box shadow

```
<style>
  .shadow {
    box-shadow: 5px 5px black;
    background: #CCCCCC;
    width: 10rem;
    height: 5rem;
  }
</style>

<div class="shadow"></div>
```

Figure 4-13. *The rendered result*

We can also add a blur radius to blur the shadow, as demonstrated in Listing 4-10. The result is shown in Figure 4-14.

Listing 4-10. Adding a blur radius

```
<style>
  .shadow {
    box-shadow: 5px 5px 10px black;
    background: #CCCCCC;
    width: 10rem;
    height: 5rem;
  }
</style>

<div class="shadow"></div>
```

Figure 4-14. *The rendered shadow with a blur radius*

If we add a spread radius and set the blur radius to zero, as shown in Listing 4-11, we can see that the shadow size grows by the spread radius in all directions. The result is shown in Figure 4-15.

Listing 4-11. Adding a spread radius without a blur radius

```
<style>
  .shadow {
    box-shadow: 5px 5px 0 5px black;
    background: #CCCCCC;
    width: 10rem;
    height: 5rem;
  }
</style>

<div class="shadow"></div>
```

Figure 4-15. *The rendered shadow*

Finally, we can apply the blur radius again to see the full result.

Listing 4-12. Shadow with a blur and spread radius

```
<style>
  .shadow {
    box-shadow: 5px 5px 10px 5px black;
    background: #CCCCCC;
    width: 10rem;
    height: 5rem;
  }
</style>

<div class="shadow"></div>
```

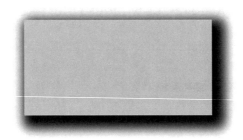

Figure 4-16. *The full rendered shadow*

We could also set the X and Y offsets to zero, as shown in Listing 4-13, and let the shadow spread and blur evenly in all directions. The result is shown in Figure 4-17.

Listing 4-13. Setting the X and Y offsets to zero

```
<style>
  .shadow {
    box-shadow: 0 0 5px 5px black;
    background: #CCCCCC;
    width: 10rem;
    height: 5rem;
  }
</style>

<div class="shadow"></div>
```

Figure 4-17. *The rendered result*

Box shadows can also be inside the element instead of behind it. To do this, specify the inset keyword, as shown in Listing 4-14. The result is shown in Figure 4-18.

Listing 4-14. An inset box shadow

```
<style>
  .shadow {
    box-shadow: 0 0 25px black inset;
    background: #CCCCCC;
    width: 10rem;
    height: 5rem;
  }
</style>

<div class="shadow"></div>
```

Figure 4-18. *The rendered result*

Finally, you can apply multiple shadows to an element, as shown in Listing 4-15. This could be used, for example, to apply both an inner and outer shadow. The resulting shadows are shown in Figure 4-19.

Listing 4-15. Multiple box shadows

```
<style>
  .shadow {
    box-shadow: 0 0 10px 0 black, 0 0 25px red inset;
    background: #CCCCCC;
    width: 10rem;
    height: 5rem;
  }
</style>

<div class="shadow"></div>
```

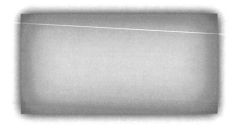

Figure 4-19. *The rendered result, showing two box shadows*

Opacity

By default, most elements start out with a transparent background. When a background color or image is assigned, that element becomes opaque. You cannot see through the element to what's behind it. Borders and text are also opaque.

You can change this behavior with the opacity property. opacity applies to the entire element – background, border, text, images, and any other content within that element or its children.

The opacity property takes a number between 0 and 1 or a percentage from 0% to 100%. This sets the level of transparency of the element. An opacity of 0.5, or 50%, is half transparent. Listing 4-16 shows an example of setting opacity. The result is shown in Figure 4-20.

Listing 4-16. Demonstration of opacity

```
<style>
  .outer {
    background: red;
    height: 10rem;
    width: 10rem;
  }

  .inner {
    background: blue;
    color: white;
    height: 8rem;
    width: 8rem;
    opacity: 0.5;
  }
</style>

<div class="outer">
  <div class="inner">
    Hello World!
  </div>
</div>
```

Figure 4-20. *The rendered result*

Notice that the red background of the outer box partially shows through the inner box and its text. If we set opacity to `0.2`, the inner box becomes even more transparent and is barely visible, as shown in Figure 4-21.

Figure 4-21. *Decreasing the opacity*

Hiding elements

There are a few ways you can hide an element on the page using CSS.

display: none

When the `display` property is set to `none`, the element is removed from the flow of the document as if it was never there. Other elements will move to fill in the space.

Consider the example shown in Figure 4-22.

Figure 4-22. *Three boxes*

If we set the blue middle element's `display` property to `none`, it is removed, and the other block moves to the left to fill the empty space, as shown in Figure 4-23.

Figure 4-23. *The middle element hidden with* `display: none`

visibility: hidden

Another way to hide an element is by setting the `visibility` property to `hidden`. This behaves a little differently than `display: none` – the flow of the document is not affected. This means that no elements will move to fill the empty space left by the hidden element.

If we change the middle box from Figure 4-22 to `visibility: hidden`, it will disappear, but an empty space will remain, as shown in Figure 4-24.

Figure 4-24. *The empty space left by* `visibility: hidden`

To restore the hidden element, we can set the `visibility` property back to `visible`.

opacity: 0

The last way to hide an element is to set its `opacity` property to 0. This has the same net effect as `visibility: hidden` – the element is effectively hidden, but the layout is unchanged. To show the element again, just set `opacity` back to 1.

One reason you may want to use `opacity: 0` instead of `visibility: hidden` is while the `visibility` property will show or hide the element immediately, the `opacity` property can be transitioned gradually with a CSS transition, which we'll learn more about in Chapter 9. This can be used to create a subtle fade-in/fade-out effect.

Summary

In this chapter, we learned about some of the basic styling techniques with CSS:

- A border has a style, width, and color.

- Rounded corners can be created with the `border-radius` property.

- An element can have an inner and/or outer box shadow.

- The `opacity` property determines the transparency of an element.

- An element can be hidden in three ways: `display: none`, `visibility: hidden`, or `opacity: 0`.

CHAPTER 5

Backgrounds and Gradients

Any HTML element can have a background. Backgrounds can be images, solid colors, or even gradients.

Solid background colors

Solid background colors are applied using the background-color property. This accepts any valid CSS color expression.

Listing 5-1. A solid background color

```
<style>
  .red-background {
    background-color: #FF0000;
  }
</style>

<div class="red-background">Hello world!</div>
```

Hello world!

Figure 5-1. *The rendered result*

Background images

Images can also be used as an element's background. There are several properties that control the background image.

© Joe Attardi 2020
J. Attardi, *Modern CSS*, https://doi.org/10.1007/978-1-4842-6294-8_5

background-image

One or more background images can be applied using the background-image property. This accepts one or more image URLs. The background images will be stacked on top of each other, with the first image on top.

A background image's URL is specified with the url function. It takes one argument, which is a string that can be an absolute or relative URL. Here are a few examples:

- Absolute URL: url('https://imgur.com/my-image.png');

- Relative URL: url('/header.png');

Listing 5-2. Using a background image

```
<style>
  .background-image {
    background-image: url('tiles.jpg');
    height: 5rem;
    width: 10rem;
  }
</style>

<div class="background-image"></div>
```

Figure 5-2. _The rendered result_

background-repeat

If an element is larger than its background image, by default the image will be repeated to fill the element.

Listing 5-3. Using a background image on an element larger than the image itself

```
<style>
  .background-image {
    background-image: url(tiles.jpg);
    height: 50rem;
    width: 100rem;
  }
</style>

<div class="background-image"></div>
```

Figure 5-3. *The tiled background image*

This behavior can be changed with the background-repeat property. Repeating can be disabled by setting it to no-repeat. If the background isn't repeated to cover the entire element, the background color, if any, will show through.

Listing 5-4. Disabling background repeat

```
<style>
  .background-image {
    background-color: #999999;
    background-image: url('tiles.jpg');
```

```
    background-repeat: no-repeat;
    height: 50rem;
    width: 100rem;
  }
</style>

<div class="background-image"></div>
```

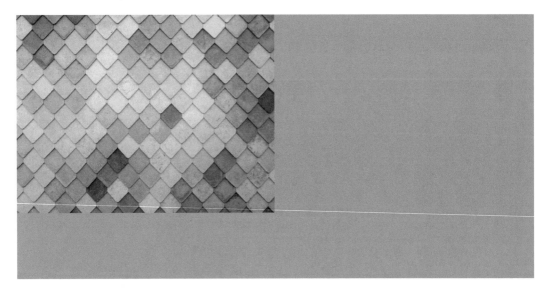

Figure 5-4. *The rendered result*

The background image can be repeated just horizontally or just vertically by specifying a background-repeat of repeat-x or repeat-y.

Listing 5-5. Repeating the background vertically only

```
<style>
  .background-image {
    background-color: #999999;
    background-image: url('tiles.jpg');
    background-repeat: repeat-y;
    height: 50rem;
```

```
    width: 100rem;
  }
</style>

<div class="background-image"></div>
```

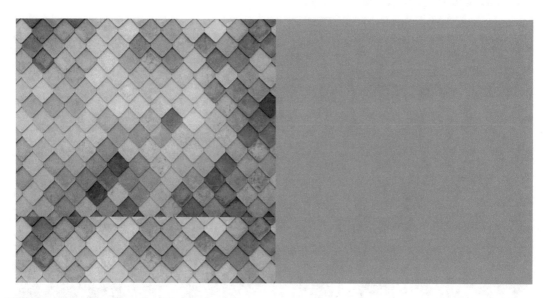

Figure 5-5. *The rendered result*

background-position

The position of the background image can be changed with the background-position property.

Listing 5-6. The background-position property

```
<style>
  .background-image {
    background-color: #999999;
    background-image: url('tiles.jpg');
    background-repeat: no-repeat;
    background-position: center;
```

```
    height: 50rem;
    width: 100rem;
  }
</style>

<div class="background-image"></div>
```

Figure 5-6. *The rendered result*

A single value can be given such as top, bottom, left, right, or center, a length such as 50px, or a percentage. Two values can also be given. In this case, the first value is the position along the X-axis, and the second is the position along the Y-axis.

Listing 5-7. Specifying two values for background-position

```
<style>
  .background-image {
    background-color: #999999;
    background-image: url('tiles.jpg');
    background-repeat: no-repeat;
    background-position: 50px center;
    height: 50rem;
    width: 100rem;
  }
```

```
</style>

<div class="background-image"></div>
```

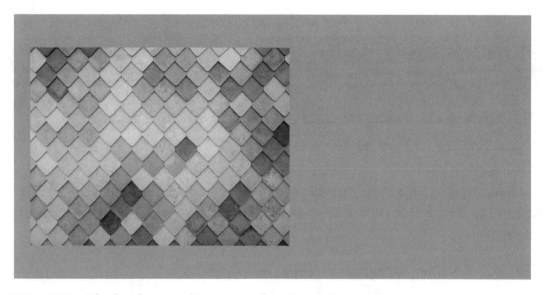

Figure 5-7. *The background image in the specified position*

background-size

By default, the background image will have its original size. This may not always be ideal and can be changed with the background-size property. Consider this example where the element is wider than the background image being used.

Listing 5-8. An element wider than its background image

```
<style>
  .header-image {
    background-image: url('mountains.jpg');
    height: 15rem;
    border: 3px solid #000000;
  }
</style>
```

```
<div class="header-image">
  <h1>Welcome to my site</h1>
</div>
```

Figure 5-8. *The background image is tiled*

Since the element is wider than its background, the background is tiled, as we saw before. This doesn't look good, though. Just like before, we can set background-repeat to no-repeat.

Listing 5-9. Setting background-repeat to no-repeat

```
<style>
  .header-image {
    background-image: url('mountains.jpg');
    background-repeat: no-repeat;
    height: 15rem;
    border: 3px solid #000000;
  }
</style>

<div class="header-image">
  <h1>Welcome to my site</h1>
</div>
```

This fixes the tiling issue but creates a new issue. There is a big white gap inside the element between the background image and the border.

Figure 5-9. *A gap inside the element*

We can improve this further by setting the background-size property to cover. This will resize the background image to make sure that the element is fully covered. If the aspect ratio of the image doesn't match that of the element, the image will be cropped.

Listing 5-10. Setting background-size to cover

```
<style>
  .header-image {
    background-image: url('mountains.jpg');
    background-size: cover;
    height: 15rem;
    border: 3px solid #000000;
  }
</style>

<div class="header-image">
  <h1>Welcome to my site</h1>
</div>
```

Figure 5-10. *The rendered result*

This looks better. The background fills the element without tiling or a gap. It's still not ideal, though. Most of the image is cut off – we don't see the mountains, which are the focal point of the image.

To fix this, we can combine the `background-position` property with `background-size`, setting the position to `center` to focus on the center of the image.

Listing 5-11. Focusing on the center of the background image

```
<style>
  .header-image {
    background-image: url('mountains.jpg');
    background-size: cover;
    background-position: center;
    height: 15rem;
    border: 3px solid #000000;
  }
</style>

<div class="header-image">
  <h1>Welcome to my site</h1>
</div>
```

Now, we get a much nicer result. The mountains at the center of the background image are visible.

Figure 5-11. *A better view of the background image*

There are some other useful values for `background-size` as well. One such value is `contain`, which will resize the background image so that the entire image fits within the element.

Figure 5-12. *Setting background-size to contain*

You can also set a specific size in pixels, which can cause strange results if the aspect ratio is not preserved.

Listing 5-12. Setting a specific background size

```
<style>
  .header-image {
    background-image: url('mountains.jpg');
    background-size: 100px 300px;
    height: 15rem;
    border: 3px solid #000000;
  }
</style>

<div class="header-image">
  <h1>Welcome to my site</h1>
</div>
```

Because the given dimensions are not the same aspect ratio as the original image, it appears squashed in the horizontal direction, as seen in Figure 5-13.

Figure 5-13. *The rendered result*

background-clip

By default, an element's background goes behind its border, padding, and content. If we add some padding to the header image, and change the border, we can see that behavior.

Listing 5-13. Adding padding and changing border

```
<style>
  .header-image {
    background-image: url('mountains.jpg');
    background-size: cover;
    background-position: center;
    height: 15rem;
    border: 5px dashed #000000;
    padding: 2rem;
  }
</style>

<div class="header-image">
  <h1>Welcome to my site</h1>
</div>
```

This behavior can be changed with the `background-clip` property. It can take the following values.

border-box

The background will extend all the way to the border, as shown in Figure 5-14. This is the default behavior.

Figure 5-14. *The background is behind the border and padding areas*

padding-box

The background will extend to the padding area, but will not appear behind the border, as shown in Figure 5-15.

Figure 5-15. *The background does not extend behind the border*

content-box

The background will only be shown behind the content area. It will not extend into the padding area or the border, as shown in Figure 5-16.

Figure 5-16. *The background only extends into the content area*

background

Finally, there is also a `background` shorthand property that lets you set several of these properties in a single value. A background color can also be included. The values can be given in any order, with a few exceptions:

- The `background-size` must come directly after `background-position`, separated by a slash.

- The `background-color` must come last.

Listing 5-14. The background shorthand property

```
<style>
  .header-image {
    background: url('mountains.jpg') center / cover;
    height: 15rem;
    border: 3px solid #000000;
  }
</style>

<div class="header-image">
  <h1>Welcome to my site</h1>
</div>
```

Gradients

In addition to solid colors and images, CSS also supports gradient backgrounds. In the past, this was achieved by creating an image containing the desired gradient and setting that as a background-image. With modern browsers, and even IE11, this is no longer needed, as gradients are natively supported.

There are two types of gradients supported in all browsers:

- *Linear gradients* go along a straight line. They can go left to right, top to bottom, or at an arbitrary angle.

- *Radial gradients* start at a central point and radiate outward.

There is no CSS property for gradients; they are treated as background images. Gradients are specified with the linear-gradient and radial-gradient functions in the value for the background-image property.

Linear gradients

A linear gradient gradually transitions between colors along a straight line. A gradient can have multiple "stops" or color transitions. Listing 5-15 shows the simplest possible linear gradient.

Listing 5-15. A simple linear gradient

```
<style>
  .gradient {
    background-image: linear-gradient(red, blue);
    width: 10rem;
    height: 5rem;
  }
</style>

<div class="gradient"></div>
```

By default, a linear gradient goes from top to bottom, and the stops are evenly distributed. The gradient in Figure 5-17 has two stops. The first is red, and the second is blue.

Figure 5-17. *The rendered gradient*

Adding more stops

You can easily add more stops to a linear gradient.

Listing 5-16. A gradient with three stops

```
<style>
  .gradient {
    background-image: linear-gradient(
      red,
      blue,
      green
    );
    width: 10rem;
```

```
    height: 5rem;
  }
</style>

<div class="gradient"></div>
```

Figure 5-18. *The rendered gradient*

Using transparency

You can even use transparency in a gradient.

Listing 5-17. Specifying transparent as gradient stops

```
<style>
  .gradient {
    background-image: linear-gradient(
      transparent,
      blue,
      transparent
    );
    width: 10rem;
    height: 5rem;
  }
</style>

<div class="gradient"></div>
```

Figure 5-19. *A gradient with transparent stops*

Changing the direction

To change the direction of the gradient from its default of top to bottom, add an argument of the format: to <direction> at the beginning of the linear-gradient function. This specifies the direction of the gradient.

Listing 5-18. Specifying the gradient direction

```
<style>
  .gradient {
    background-image: linear-gradient(
      to right,
      red,
      blue
    );
    width: 10rem;
    height: 5rem;
  }
</style>

<div class="gradient"></div>
```

This results in a horizontal gradient, starting from red on the left and moving to the right to blue, as shown in Figure 5-20.

Figure 5-20. *A horizontal gradient*

You can also specify an arbitrary angle for the linear gradient.

Listing 5-19. Specifying an angle for the gradient

```
<style>
  .gradient {
    background-image: linear-gradient(
      45deg,
      red,
      blue
    );
    width: 10rem;
    height: 5rem;
  }
</style>

<div class="gradient"></div>
```

The code in Listing 5-19 results in a linear gradient that starts at the bottom left corner, and moves at a 45-degree angle, as shown in Figure 5-21.

Figure 5-21. *A 45-degree gradient*

Customizing stops

So far, the linear gradients we've seen have had an even distribution of colors. The color stops were spaced equally across the gradient. You can change the position along the gradient where the color changes happen by specifying a percentage after the color stop. Listing 5-20 shows an example of this.

Listing 5-20. Customizing gradient stops

```
<style>
  .gradient {
    background-image: linear-gradient(
      to right,
      red 0%,
      blue 25%
    );
    width: 10rem;
    height: 5rem;
  }
</style>

<div class="gradient"></div>
```

Figure 5-22. *The rendered gradient*

Notice how the gradient starts with a solid red color, then gradually transitions to blue at the 25% mark.

Two adjoining stops with the same color will create a region of solid color.

Listing 5-21. A gradient with two adjacent stops of the same color

```
<style>
  .gradient {
    background-image: linear-gradient(
      to right,
      red 0%,
      green 25%,
      green 75%,
      blue 100%
    );
    width: 10rem;
    height: 5rem;
  }
</style>

<div class="gradient"></div>
```

Figure 5-23. *A gradient with a solid region in the middle*

Note that between 25% and 75%, the color is solid green. Similarly, if the first stop is after 0%, or the last stop is before 100%, the remaining space before or after will be a solid color.

In addition to percentages, color stops can be specified with any valid length value in px, em, rem, or other units.

Radial gradients

A radial gradient starts at a central point and radiates outward. Listing 5-22 has an example of a simple radial gradient.

Listing 5-22. A radial gradient

```
<style>
  .gradient {
    background-image: radial-gradient(red, blue);
    width: 10rem;
    height: 5rem;
  }
</style>

<div class="gradient"></div>
```

Figure 5-24. *The rendered radial gradient*

Customizing the shape and position

The shape of a radial gradient can be defined as an ellipse (the default), or a circle. The shape is defined as the name of the shape and a position such as top, right, left, center, or specific percentages or values. The shape is defined as <shape> at <position>. The position can be omitted, in which case it defaults to center.

Listing 5-23. Specifying a circle for the radial gradient shape

```
<style>
  .gradient {
    background-image: radial-gradient(
      circle,
      red,
      blue
    );
    width: 10rem;
```

```
    height: 5rem;
  }
</style>

<div class="gradient"></div>
```

Figure 5-25. *The circular gradient*

We can move the circle to the left by specifying a position of 25%, as demonstrated in Listing 5-24.

Listing 5-24. Specifying the position of the gradient shape

```
<style>
  .gradient {
    background-image: radial-gradient(
      circle at 25%,
      red,
      blue
    );
    width: 10rem;
    height: 5rem;
  }
</style>

<div class="gradient"></div>
```

The center of the circle in Figure 5-26 is at the 25% mark along the horizontal axis.

Figure 5-26. *The circle gradient at 25%*

Two values can also be given for the position, such as top left.

Listing 5-25. Specifying two values for the position

```
<style>
  .gradient {
    background-image: radial-gradient(
      circle at top left,
      red,
      blue
    );
    width: 10rem;
    height: 5rem;
  }
</style>

<div class="gradient"></div>
```

Figure 5-27. *The circle gradient in the top-left corner*

Customizing the size

The size of the gradient can be further influenced by providing modifiers to the shape that define where the gradient should end. The options that can be set are

- closest-side: The gradient ends at the side closest to the center of the gradient. For a wide rectangle, this would be the top or bottom.

- farthest-side: The gradient ends at the side farthest from the center of the gradient. For a wide rectangle, this would be the left or right.

- closest-corner: The gradient ends at the closest corner to its center.

- farthest-corner: The gradient ends at the farthest corner from its center. This is the default.

Customizing stops

A radial gradient can also have multiple color stops.

Listing 5-26. A radial gradient with multiple color stops

```
<style>
  .gradient {
    background-image: radial-gradient(
      red,
      blue,
      green 75%
    );
    width: 10rem;
    height: 5rem;
  }
</style>

<div class="gradient"></div>
```

Figure 5-28. *The rendered gradient*

Multiple gradients

You can even combine multiple radial gradients applied to an element if you use a transparent color as one of the stops.

Listing 5-27. Multiple gradients

```
<style>
  .gradient {
    background-image: radial-gradient(
      ellipse at 25%,
      red,transparent
    ), radial-gradient(
      ellipse at 75%,
      blue,
      transparent
    );
    width: 10rem;
    height: 5rem;
  }
</style>

<div class="gradient"></div>
```

Figure 5-29. *The rendered gradients*

Combining backgrounds

Gradients and background images can be combined to achieve light and shadow effects. Listing 5-28 has an example of applying a lighting effect with a gradient that goes from white to transparent.

Listing 5-28. Applying a lighting effect with a gradient

```
<style>
  .header-image {
    background-image:
      radial-gradient(
        ellipse at top left,
        white 25%,
        transparent
      ),
      url('mountains.jpg');
    background-size: cover;
    background-position: center;
    height: 15rem;
  }
</style>

<div class="header-image"></div>
```

Similarly, a shadow effect could be achieved by using a dark color such as gray or black instead of white.

Figure 5-30. *The rendered result*

Summary

In this chapter, we learned

- An element's background can be a solid color, an image, a gradient, or a combination of the three.

- The display of a background image can be customized with the `background-repeat`, `background-position`, `background-size`, and `background-clip` properties.

- Gradients can be linear or radial.

- Gradients can be combined with background images or colors.

CHAPTER 6

Text Styling

Now that we've covered the basics of styling, let's explore the styling of text.

Fonts

You can use any font installed on your system for styling your website, but you should use a web-safe font. These are fonts that are generally considered safe to use because they are available on most users' systems.

Table 6-1 shows the generally accepted web-safe fonts along with their generic font family names.

Table 6-1. *Web-safe fonts*

Font	Family
Arial	`sans-serif`
Trebuchet MS	
Verdana	
Courier New	`monospace`
Georgia	`serif`
Times New Roman	

Basic text styling

There are several CSS properties that control basic text styling. We'll discuss a few of them in this section.

font-family

The `font-family` property sets the font to use for the element's text. This font is inherited by descendant elements.

© Joe Attardi 2020
J. Attardi, *Modern CSS*, https://doi.org/10.1007/978-1-4842-6294-8_6

`font-family` can be specified as a single value, the name of the font to use. More commonly, a comma-separated list of fonts is given. The browser will try each font, starting with the first, until a match is found. Generally, the list starts specific and gets more general. The last font family in the list is typically a generic one like `monospace` or `sans-serif`, where the browser will use a fallback font that approximates the desired appearance. Font names containing spaces should be enclosed in quotes, as shown in Listing 6-1.

Listing 6-1. Specifying multiple font names

```
.hello {
  font-family:
    Georgia,
    'Times New Roman',
    serif;
}
```

In this example, the browser will try Georgia first. If Georgia is unavailable, it will try Times New Roman. Lastly, if that is not available, it will fall back to a built-in generic serif font. Custom web fonts can also be used. We will discuss that a little later.

font-size

An element inherits its parent's font size by default. This behavior can be overridden by using the `font-size` property, which sets the font size for the element. Recall that the document has a base font size - usually `16px`. The value of `font-size` not only controls the size of the text, but it also determines base sizing for anything specified in em or other relative units. The em unit is not just for text. Borders, padding, and even width and height, can all be specified in ems.

In addition, there are several predefined `font-size` values, ranging from `xx-small` to `xxx-large`. A relative font size can also be specified, with a value of `smaller` or `larger`. A `font-size` can also be specified as a percentage of its parent's size.

As mentioned in Chapter 3, a `font-size` specified in em units has a compounding effect if its children also use em units. Listing 6-2 shows an example of this effect.

Listing 6-2. Using em units on the parent and child

```
<style>
  .parent {
    font-size: 1.5em;
  }

  .child {
    font-size: 1.5em;
  }
</style>

<div class="parent">
  I'm the parent
  <div class="child">
    I'm the child
  </div>
</div>
```

I'm the parent
I'm the child

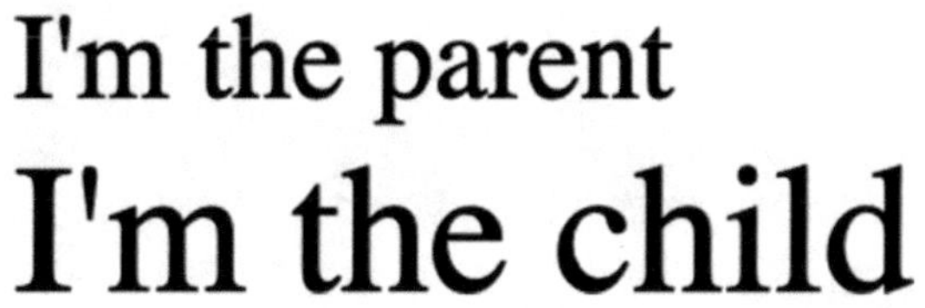

Figure 6-1. *The parent and child have different font sizes*

Note that while the parent and child elements both have a `font-size` of `1.5em`, the child's text is larger. This is the compounding effect. The parent's font size is `1.5em`, or 1.5 times its parent's font size, which is the root element's font size of 16px. This comes out to 24px.

The child element's font size is also `1.5em`, 1.5 times of its parent, which we just calculated to be 24px. 24px * 1.5 = 36px.

If we used `rem` units for the parent and child, they would have the same font size because rem is relative to the *root element*'s font size.

color

The color property controls the element's text color (and *text decorations* such as underlines). It also sets the *current color*. This is a special value called currentColor that resolves to the text color, which can be referenced from other properties. currentColor is also the default border color, if one is not specified. Listing 6-3 has an example of color and currentColor in action.

Listing 6-3. The color value and currentColor property

```
<style>
  div {
    border: 3px solid currentColor;
  }

  .one {
    color: red;
  }

  .two {
    color: blue;
  }
</style>

<div class="one">One</div>
<div class="two">Two</div>
```

We gave one element a color of red and the other a color of blue. This set the currentColor value of each element. Then, we also had a rule that selected both div elements and used the currentColor as the border color. The red div gets a red border, and the blue div gets a blue border.

Figure 6-2. *The rendered result*

font-weight

The `font-weight` property defines how bold the text appears. This can be a simple value like `normal` or `bold`. It can also take numeric values: 100, 200, 300, 400, 500, 600, 700, 800, and 900. The higher the number, the bolder the font is. The `normal` value is equivalent to a weight of 400, and the `bold` value is equivalent to a weight of 700. Depending on the font used, not all weights may be available.

`font-weight` can also be specified as the values `lighter` or `bolder`. These values are relative to the weight of the element's parent.

font-style

The `font-style` property can be used to make text italic. It has three supported values: `normal`, `italic`, and `oblique`. Italic and oblique are similar but slightly different. *Italic* is typically an angled font face, sometimes with a completely different design than the normal version. On the other hand, *oblique* is typically just the normal version, slanted.

Not all fonts include both an italic and oblique version. In this case, the italic and oblique styles look the same.

text-decoration

The `text-decoration` property can be used to add decorative lines to text. These can be underlines, strikethrough lines, and even wavy lines (on most browsers).

The basic usage of `text-decoration` takes a simple value: `none`, `underline`, or `line-through`.

Listing 6-4. Demonstrating the basic usage of `text-decoration`

```
<style>
  .underline {
    text-decoration: underline;
  }

  .strikethrough {
    text-decoration: line-through;
  }
```

```
  .none {
    text-decoration: none;
  }
</style>

<div class="underline">Underlined text</div>
<div class="strikethrough">Strikethrough text</div>
<div class="none">No text decoration</div>
```

Underlined text
~~Strikethrough text~~
No text decoration

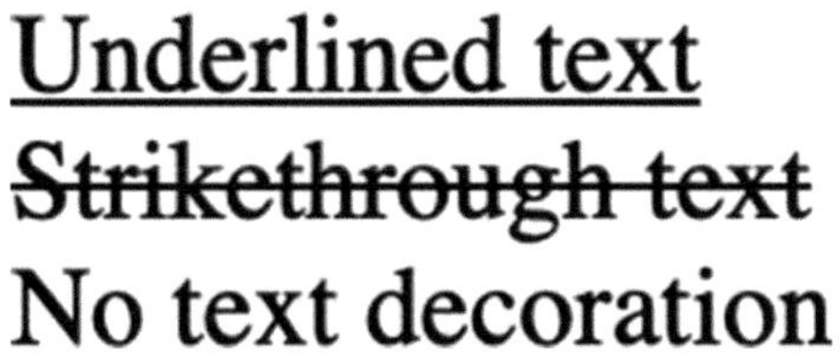

Figure 6-3. *The different text decoration types*

The text-decoration property can also take a color and a style. The available styles are solid, double, dotted, dashed, and wavy.

Listing 6-5. The different options for text decoration style

```
<style>
  div {
    font-size: 2rem;
  }

  .solid {
    text-decoration: underline solid blue;
  }

  .double {
    text-decoration: underline double green;
  }

  .dotted {
    text-decoration: underline dotted;
  }
```

```
  .dashed {
    text-decoration: underline dashed purple;
  }

  .wavy {
    text-decoration: underline wavy red;
  }
</style>

<div class="solid">Solid blue underline</div>
<div class="double">Double green underline</div>
<div class="dotted">Dotted black underline</div>
<div class="dashed">Dashed purple underline</div>
<div class="wavy">Wavy red underline</div>
```

The different rendered styles can be seen in Figure 6-4.

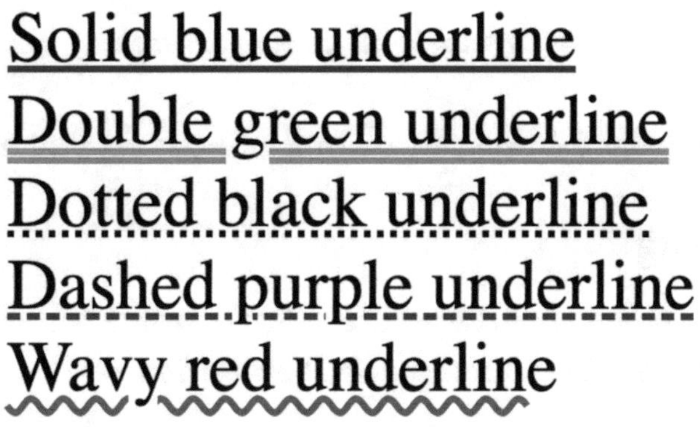

<u>Solid blue underline</u>
<u>Double green underline</u>
<u>Dotted black underline</u>
<u>Dashed purple underline</u>
<u>Wavy red underline</u>

Figure 6-4. *The various text decoration styles*

Some elements, such as links, have an underline by default. This can be removed by setting text-decoration to none.

Compatibility note   In Internet Explorer 11, only the basic usage of text-decoration is supported. That is, text-decoration can be set to none, underline, or line-through. Colors and styles are not supported.

Other text effects

text-transform

The text-transform property can be used to transform the text to all uppercase.

Listing 6-6. Example usage of the text-transform property

```
<style>
  .hello {
    text-transform: uppercase;
  }
</style>

<div class="hello">Hello world!</div>
```

HELLO WORLD!

Figure 6-5. *The text is transformed to all uppercase letters*

Some of the other values for text-transform are none, capitalize, and lowercase.

letter-spacing

The letter-spacing property can be used to adjust the space between each letter. The specified value is added to the normal spacing between letters.

Listing 6-7. Example usage of the letter-spacing property

```
<style>
  .hello {
    letter-spacing: 5px;
  }
</style>

<div class="hello">Hello world!</div>
```

Hello world!

Figure 6-6. *The letters are spaced an extra 5px apart*

font-variant

The font-variant property can be set to small-caps for an interesting effect. All lowercase letters are transformed into smaller-sized capital letters.

Listing 6-8. Example usage of the font-variant property

```
<style>
  .hello {
    font-variant: small-caps;
  }
</style>

<div class="hello">Hello world!</div>
```

HELLO WORLD!

Figure 6-7. *The rendered text with small caps*

Text layout

In addition to styling, there are also several useful properties that affect the text layout.

text-indent

The text-indent property is used to specify an indent on the first line of text in a block element.

Listing 6-9. Example usage of the text-indent property

```
<style>
  .my-text {
```

```
    border: 1px solid red;
    text-indent: 50px;
    width: 10rem;
  }
</style>

<div class="my-text">Here is a brief paragraph that has enough content to
wrap a few lines.</div>
```

```
            Here is a brief
paragraph that has
enough content to wrap
a few lines.
```

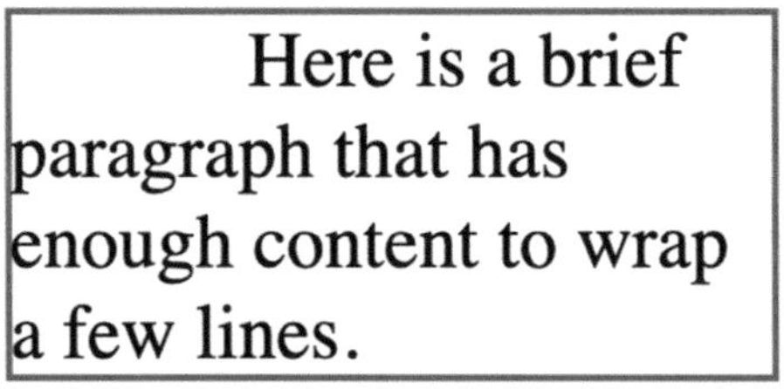

Figure 6-8. *The first line of text in the paragraph is indented by 50px*

white-space

The white-space property is used to specify how whitespace is handled inside an element that contains text. The default value is normal. With this value, sequential whitespace characters are collapsed. If the text content exceeds the width of its container, it will be wrapped to the next line.

You may have seen this behavior before, when you have multiple consecutive spaces in your HTML, or line breaks, and they are ignored by the browser.

Listing 6-10. An example with extra whitespace

```
<style>
  .my-text {
    border: 1px solid red;
    width: 10rem;
  }
</style>

<div class="my-text">
```

```
Here is some text
    with
        whitespace.
</div>
```

Here is some text with
whitespace.

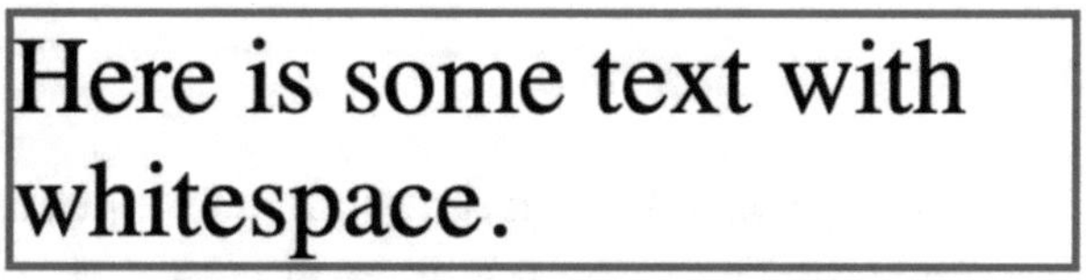

Figure 6-9. *The whitespace is ignored*

The extra spaces and line breaks were ignored, and the text only breaks to the next line when it automatically wraps.

We can make the browser respect the whitespace by setting white-space to pre.

Listing 6-11. Setting white-space to pre

```
<style>
  .my-text {
    border: 1px solid red;
    width: 10rem;
    white-space: pre;
  }
</style>

<div class="my-text">
  Here is some text
    with
        whitespace.
</div>
```

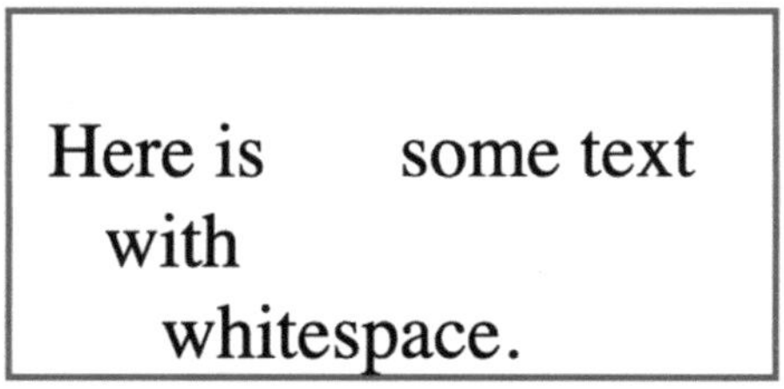

Figure 6-10. *The whitespace is preserved*

Notice how the whitespace is preserved in the rendered output now. You might also notice that there is an extra blank line at the top of the element. This represents the first line break after the opening `div` tag.

When `white-space` is set to `pre`, lines of text are not automatically wrapped. Some other accepted values for the `white-space` property are

- `normal`: The default behavior. Whitespace is collapsed, and text is automatically wrapped as needed.

- `nowrap`: Same as `normal`, except that lines of text do not wrap.

- `pre-wrap`: Same as `pre`, except that lines of text are also wrapped.

- `pre-line`: Same as `pre-wrap`, except that consecutive whitespace characters are collapsed. Line breaks are still preserved.

- `break-spaces`: Same as `pre-wrap`, except that line wrapping behavior is slightly different. *Not supported in Internet Explorer.*

Truncating text

Your design may require that text must fit within its container without overflowing or wrapping. This can easily be accomplished by using the `white-space`, `overflow`, and `text-overflow` properties together.

First, `white-space` is set to `nowrap`. This ensures the text does not wrap but will in turn cause the text to overflow the container. By setting `overflow` to `hidden`, we can hide the overflowing content. However, then the text is abruptly cut off at the end of the container. Finally, we can set `text-overflow` to `ellipsis` to truncate the text and add an ellipsis at the end.

Listing 6-12. Truncating text

```
<style>
  .my-text {
    border: 1px solid red;
    overflow: hidden;
    text-overflow: ellipsis;
    white-space: nowrap;
    width: 10rem;
  }
</style>

<div class="my-text">Here is a really really long string.</div>
```

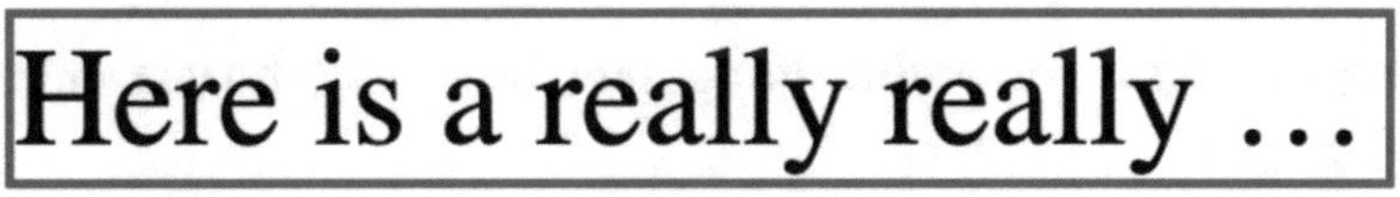

Here is a really really ...

Figure 6-11. *The overflowing text is truncated with an ellipsis*

line-height

The line-height property controls the height of each line of text. It can be used to add spacing between lines of text.

Horizontal alignment

Horizontal alignment is controlled by the text-align property. This only has an effect on block elements with a width greater than that of their content. Valid values are left, right, center, and justify.

Listing 6-13. Setting the text alignment

```
<style>
  .hello {
    border: 2px solid red;
    width: 30rem;
```

```
    text-align: center;
  }
</style>

<div class="hello">Hello world!</div>
```

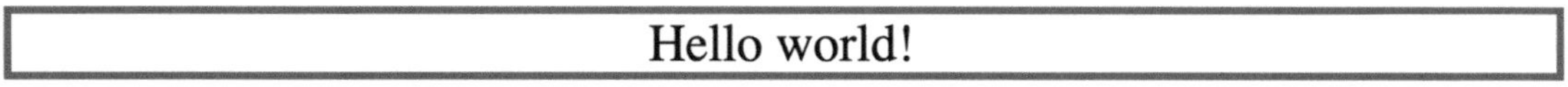

> Hello world!

Figure 6-12. *The text is horizontally centered*

text-align doesn't just affect text. It sets the horizontal alignment of any inline element inside the containing element on which text-align is set.

Vertical alignment

If a block element's height is taller than its content, by default the text will be aligned to the top of the container.

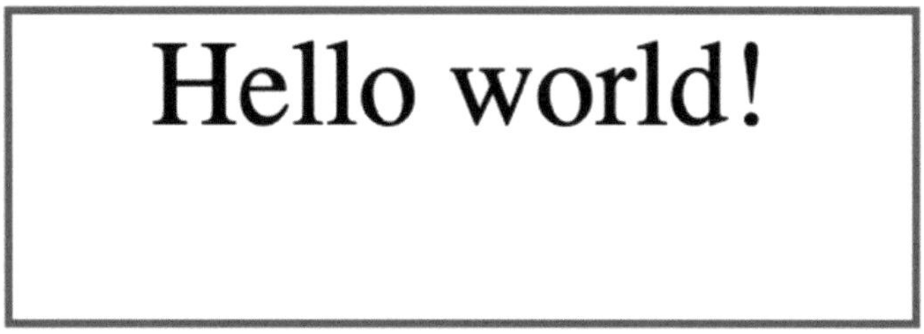

Hello world!

Figure 6-13. *The text defaults to top vertical alignment*

You might think the vertical-align property would help here but setting vertical-align: center would have no effect. One way to solve this problem is to set the line-height to the same as the container height, as shown in Listing 6-14.

Listing 6-14. Vertically centering text with the line-height property

```
<style>
  .hello {
    border: 2px solid red;
    width: 15rem;
```

```
    height: 5rem;
    line-height: 5rem;
    font-size: 2rem;
    text-align: center;
  }
</style>

<div class="hello">Hello world!</div>
```

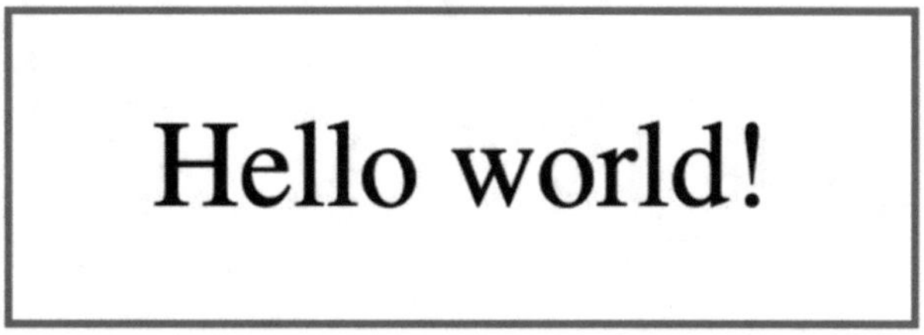

Figure 6-14. *The text is vertically centered*

How does the `vertical-align` property work, then? It controls how inline elements are aligned vertically with each other. Listing 6-15 contains two `span` elements side by side with different heights inside a container element.

Listing 6-15. Two span elements

```
<style>
  .container {
    border: 2px dashed blue;
    width: 20rem;
    text-align: center;
  }
  .hello {
    border: 2px solid red;
    font-size: 2rem;
  }
  .world {
    border: 2px solid red;
```

```
    font-size: 4rem;
  }
</style>

<div class="container">
  <span class="hello">Hello</span>
  <span class="world">World!</span>
</div>
```

Figure 6-15. *The rendered result*

In Figure 6-15, we can see that the elements are aligned along their baselines. A baseline is an invisible line along which most letters sit. If we set vertical-align to middle on both elements, they become vertically aligned with each other.

Listing 6-16. Setting vertical-align to middle

```
<style>
  .container {
    border: 2px dashed blue;
    width: 20rem;
    text-align: center;
  }

  .hello {
    border: 2px solid red;
    font-size: 2rem;
    vertical-align: middle;
  }

  .world {
    border: 2px solid red;
    font-size: 4rem;
```

```
        vertical-align: middle;
    }
</style>

<div class="container">
    <span class="hello">Hello</span>
    <span class="world">World!</span>
</div>
```

Figure 6-16. *The elements are vertically aligned*

Using web fonts

If you don't want to use the web-safe fonts (and who wants to see *another* website in Arial or Times New Roman!), you are in luck. Web fonts allow the CSS to link to a font file that the browser can download. By using a web font, you can have a much more consistent look – plus, there are many beautiful web fonts out there that will enhance the look of your site or app.

There are several different supported web font formats:

- Web Open Font Format version 1 or 2 (WOFF/WOFF2)

- Embedded Open Type (EOT)

- TrueType Font (TTF)

- Scalable Vector Graphics (SVG)

Modern browsers support WOFF and WOFF2. The other font formats are for support with older browsers. A web font is typically packaged in several different formats, all of which can be referenced in the CSS.

@font-face

A web font is registered using the @font-face at-rule. A @font-face rule declares a new font. The desired name of the font is given with the font-family property, and one or more source URLs are given with the src property. Each source URL is followed by a format declaration which tells the browser which font format to expect for that file.

Once you have declared the font in a @font-face rule, you can then use the name you gave it in any font-family property in a CSS rule.

The example in Listing 6-17 will load the SomeWebFont font in WOFF2 and WOFF formats and set it as the font for the whole document. You should still provide a list of fallback fonts in case the font is not supported by the user's browser or could not be loaded.

Listing 6-17. Using a web font

```
@font-face {
  font-family: 'SomeWebFont';
  src:
    url('/some-font.woff2') format('woff2'),
    url('/some-font.woff') format('woff');
}

body {
  font-family: SomeWebFont, Arial, sans-serif;
}
```

Declaring different web font styles

Usually, a given web font file is only a single weight or style version of the font. This means there is one font file for the normal version and another for the bold version. They both must be registered in a separate @font-face rule under the same font-family. The font weight and style are specified via the font-weight and font-style properties. This is shown in Listing 6-18.

Listing 6-18. Defining two weights of a web font

```
@font-face {
  font-family: 'SomeWebFont';
  src: url('/some-font.woff2') format('woff2');
  font-weight: 400;
}

@font-face {
  font-family: 'SomeWebFont';
  src: url('/some-font-bold.woff2') format('woff2');
  font-weight: 700;
}
```

Flash of unstyled/invisible text

Like any other resource, the browser must download the web font files before they can be used. If this is not done quickly, the browser may render the site in a fallback font while the web font is still loading. Once the font is loaded, the text is re-rendered in the new font. This results in unstyled text briefly appearing before being replaced by the correctly styled text – the so-called flash of unstyled text.

Some browsers will also hide the text (up to several seconds) until the font is loaded. This results in a different, but even more annoying, phenomenon – the "flash of invisible text."

The main issue with this is that the page may reflow once the font is loaded. If the user had already started reading the text rendered in the system fallback font, they may lose their place, and it can be jarring.

One way to address this issue is to use a tool like the Web Font Loader (`https://github.com/typekit/webfontloader`), a JavaScript library that manages the loading of web fonts. This tool gives you greater control over how fonts are used during the loading process. For example, a different fallback font that looks more similar to the actual font can be used, rather than the fallback used by the browser.

This will still result in a flash of unstyled text, however, which can affect the page layout. However, with Web Font Loader, you can also tweak the `font-size` and `line-height` of the fallback font. This can result in a smoother experience.

The flash of unstyled text can't be completely solved, but its severity can be greatly reduced by using a library like Web Font Loader.

A word of caution

Web fonts are great, but don't go overboard. The more fonts that are loaded, the longer the page takes to load, and the worse the flash of unstyled text can be. You should make sure to use only the web fonts that you absolutely need.

Text shadow

The `text-shadow` property allows you to add shadows to text. It works similarly to the `box-shadow` property we saw earlier. A text shadow has X and Y offsets, an optional blur radius, and a color. Unlike `box-shadow`, `text-shadow` does not have a spread radius.

Here are some examples of text shadows. Listing 6-19 uses a shadow with an offset but no blur.

Listing 6-19. A text shadow example

```
<style>
  .container {
    font-size: 2rem;
    font-family: Arial, sans-serif;
    text-shadow: 2px 2px 0px red;
  }
</style>

<div class="container">Hello World!</div>
```

Hello World!

Figure 6-17. *The rendered text with shadow*

Listing 6-20 has another example of a text shadow, this time with no offset and a blur.

Listing 6-20. A second text shadow example

```
<style>
  .container {
    font-size: 2rem;
    font-family: Arial, sans-serif;
    text-shadow: 0px 0px 5px red;
  }
</style>

<div class="container">Hello World!</div>
```

Hello World!

Figure 6-18. *The rendered result*

Summary

In this chapter, we learned

- You can customize the font size, color, weight, and style of text.

- The text-decoration property can add underlines and strikethroughs.

- There are other text effect properties such as text-transform, letter-spacing, and font-variant.

- The white-space property controls how the browser renders whitespace. It can be ignored or respected.

- The vertical-align property controls how inline elements are vertically aligned with each other.

- Fonts can be downloaded by the browser and used with a @font-face rule.

- Text shadows can be applied with the text-shadow property.

CHAPTER 7

Layout and Positioning

We've looked a lot at how to style with CSS. Let's switch gears now and look at how to lay out and position elements.

Padding

The padding is the spacing between an element's content and its border. By default, most elements have zero padding. An element's padding is not inherited by its children.

Padding can be specified with any size unit or with a percentage. When padding is specified as a percentage, the value used is the given percentage of the containing block's width. Listing 7-1 has a simple example of this.

Listing 7-1. Setting a percentage value for padding

```
<style>
  .container {
    border: 1px solid red;
    width: 200px;
  }

  .inner {
    padding: 25%;
  }
</style>

<div class="container">
  <div class="inner">Hello world!</div>
</div>
```

© Joe Attardi 2020
J. Attardi, *Modern CSS*, https://doi.org/10.1007/978-1-4842-6294-8_7

Hello world!

Figure 7-1. *The rendered result*

If we examine the inner element with the browser's developer tools, we see that the padding is 50px, or 25% of 200px, as shown in Figure 7-2.

Figure 7-2. *The dimensions of the inner element*

Margin

The margin is the space between an element's border and other elements. The value of the margin property can be a size value, a percentage, or the keyword auto.

By default, most elements have no margin. An example of this is shown in Listing 7-2.

Listing 7-2. Elements with no margin

```
<style>
  .container {
    border: 5px solid red;
    width: 10rem;
  }

  .inner {
    border: 5px solid green;
  }
</style>

<div class="container">
  <div class="inner">Hello world!</div>
</div>
```

Figure 7-3. *The rendered result*

In Figure 7-3, there is no space between the red and green borders. This is because, by default, the elements have no margin. In Listing 7-3, we'll add some margin to the inner element.

Listing 7-3. Adding margin

```
<style>
  .container {
    border: 5px solid red;
    width: 10rem;
  }

  .inner {
    border: 5px solid green;
    margin: 1rem;
  }
</style>
```

```
<div class="container">
  <div class="inner">Hello world!</div>
</div>
```

Now there is a margin of 1rem between the inner and outer borders, as shown in Figure 7-4.

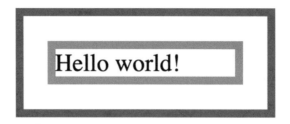

Figure 7-4. *Margin between the inner and outer borders*

Like padding, using a percentage for the margin property will set the given percentage of the containing block's width as the margin.

Centering with `margin: auto`

The margin property also accepts the auto value. When the horizontal (left and right) margin is set to auto in a block or inline-block element, the element is centered horizontally within its containing element. The element takes up the specified width, and the margin is automatically distributed evenly between the left and right margins.

However, the same is not true for vertical margin. However, as we will see later, there are several other ways to vertically center a block-level element.

Listing 7-4. Horizontally centering with margin: auto

```
<style>
  .container {
    background-color: red;
    height: 5rem;
    padding: 1rem;
    width: 20rem;
  }
```

```
  .inner {
    background-color: blue;
    height: 3rem;
    margin: auto;
    width: 5rem;
  }
</style>

<div class="container">
  <div class="inner"></div>
</div>
```

As Figure 7-5 shows, the blue box is centered horizontally due to the `margin` of `auto` but not vertically.

Figure 7-5. *The element centered horizontally*

Margin collapse

When two elements with a vertical margin meet vertically, the two margins are *collapsed* into a single margin. The size of the collapsed margin depends on the size of the two margins being collapsed. If they are the same size, then the collapsed margin will be the same size as the common margin. If they are different sizes, the collapsed margin will take the size of the larger margin.

Margin collapse applies to vertical margins only.

Another situation where the vertical margins collapse is when there is no border, padding, or other content between a parent and its child.

Listing 7-5. Demonstration of margin collapse

```
<style>
  .container {
    background: red;
    margin: 1rem;
  }

  .inner {
    background: blue;
    color: white;
    margin: 1rem;
  }
</style>

<div class="container">
  <div class="inner">Inner</div>
</div>
```

As Figure 7-6 shows, the inner element has left and right margin but not top and bottom margin, because the top and bottom margins have collapsed.

Figure 7-6. *The margins of the inner element collapse*

However, if we add padding to the container element, the margin no longer collapses, and we see that the inner element has a margin now as well.

Listing 7-6. Adding padding

```
<style>
  .container {
    background: red;
    margin: 1rem;
    padding: 1rem;
  }
```

```css
.inner {
  background: blue;
  color: white;
  margin: 1rem;
}
</style>

<div class="container">
  <div class="inner">Inner</div>
</div>
```

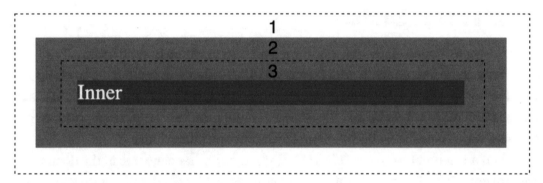

Figure 7-7. *The margin no longer collapses*

As Figure 7-7 shows, the margin no longer collapses. The numbered regions in the figure are

1. The margin of the container element

2. The padding of the container element

3. The margin of the inner element

Positioning elements

The CSS position property determines how an element is positioned. The top, right, bottom, and left properties are used in conjunction with position to determine an element's final position. The default position is static.

If an element's position property is set to any value other than static, it is considered a *positioned element*. This has important implications about the positioning of descendant elements.

position: static

static is the default value of the position property. A statically positioned element is positioned in the normal flow of the document. When position is set to static, the top, right, bottom, and left properties have no effect.

position: relative

A relatively positioned element is positioned *relative* to where it would normally appear in the flow of the document. If position is set to relative, but top, right, bottom, or left are not specified, it essentially has the same effect as if position were set to static. The one difference would be that the element would now be considered a positioned element, which can affect child elements with other position values.

When an element has a position of relative, the other elements in the document flow are not affected, even if the element has an offset. The element's original position remains in the document flow.

Listing 7-7 shows an example of a relatively positioned element.

Listing 7-7. An element with position set to relative

```
<style>
  .block {
    background-color: red;
    height: 3rem;
    width: 3rem;
  }

  .green {
    background-color: green;
  }

  .relative {
    background-color: blue;
```

```
    position: relative;
    left: 10px;
    top: 10px;
  }
</style>

<div class="block"></div>
<div class="block relative"></div>
<div class="block green"></div>
```

Figure 7-8. *The blue square is offset from its original position*

In Figure 7-8, the blue square is offset 10px below the top of its original position and 10px to the right of its original position. Note that the red and green squares remain in the same place they would be even if the blue square did not have the top and left offsets – they did not move to fill the space.

When a vertical or horizontal offset is given, the element is moved in the opposite direction. That is, top moves the element down, left moves the element to the right, right moves the element to the left, and bottom moves the element up.

What happens if you specify conflicting offsets? For example, an element can't be 10 pixels below its top position and 10 pixels above its bottom position and have the correct size. Generally, if both top and bottom are specified, the top value is used, and the bottom value is ignored. Similarly, if both left and right are specified, left wins if the text direction is left to right and right wins if the text direction is right to left.

position: absolute

An absolutely positioned element can also have top, right, bottom, and left offsets that affect its position. There are two main differences, though.

First, an absolutely positioned element is removed from the document flow and "floats" above it. The layout of other elements will be adjusted as if the absolutely positioned element is not there.

The other difference is the interpretation of the offsets. While a relatively positioned element's offsets are relative to the element's original position in the document, an absolute positioned element's offsets are relative to the *closest ancestor positioned element*. This is not necessarily the element's direct parent.

Listing 7-8 sets up an example of absolute positioning.

Listing 7-8. Three boxes inside each other

```
<style>
  .outer {
    background-color: red;
    height: 10rem;
    width: 10rem;
  }

  .inner {
    background-color: blue;
    height: 7rem;
    width: 7rem;
  }

  .core {
    background-color: green;
    height: 4rem;
    width: 4rem;
  }
</style>
```

```
<div class="outer">
  <div class="inner">
    <div class="core"></div>
  </div>
</div>
```

Figure 7-9. *The example setup*

These elements are currently all statically positioned. Let's add position: absolute to the core element and set its right property to 0.

Listing 7-9. Absolutely positioning the core element

```
<style>
  .outer {
    background-color: red;
    height: 10rem;
    width: 10rem;
  }

  .inner {
    background-color: blue;
    height: 7rem;
    width: 7rem;
  }
```

```
  .core {
    background-color: green;
    position: absolute;
    right: 0;
    height: 4rem;
    width: 4rem;
  }
</style>

<div class="outer">
  <div class="inner">
    <div class="core"></div>
  </div>
</div>
```

Figure 7-10 shows the result of this code.

Figure 7-10. *The rendered result*

This may not be what you expected. The green box is now all the way on the right-hand side of the screen. This is because it has no ancestor element that is positioned. Thus, it becomes positioned relative to the document.

Now let's add position: relative to the outer box in Listing 7-10 and see what happens.

Listing 7-10. Relatively positioning the outer box

```
<style>
  .outer {
    background-color: red;
    height: 10rem;
```

```
    width: 10rem;
    position: relative;
  }

  .inner {
    background-color: blue;
    height: 7rem;
    width: 7rem;
  }

  .core {
    background-color: green;
    position: absolute;
    right: 0;
    height: 4rem;
    width: 4rem;
  }
</style>

<div class="outer">
  <div class="inner">
    <div class="core"></div>
  </div>
</div>
```

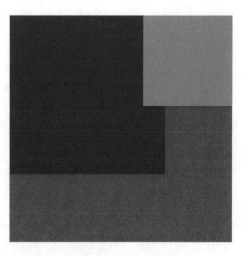

Figure 7-11. *The green box has changed position*

Now the green box is absolutely positioned relative to the outer red box, because that is the closest ancestor that is a positioned element.

Lastly, let's now relatively position the blue inner box in Listing 7-11.

Listing 7-11. Relatively positioning the inner box

```
<style>
  .outer {
    background-color: red;
    height: 10rem;
    width: 10rem;
    position: relative;
  }

  .inner {
    background-color: blue;
    position: relative;
    height: 7rem;
    width: 7rem;
  }

  .core {
    background-color: green;
    position: absolute;
    right: 0;
    height: 4rem;
    width: 4rem;
  }
</style>

<div class="outer">
  <div class="inner">
    <div class="core"></div>
  </div>
</div>
```

Figure 7-12. *The green box has moved again*

Now that the blue box is the nearest positioned ancestor of the green box, the green box is now positioned relative to the blue box.

position: fixed

Like `absolute`, a `position` of `fixed` removes the element from the document's flow. Its position is determined by setting `top`, `right`, `bottom`, and `left` properties. The difference is that for a fixed element, these offsets are always relative to the viewport. This means that even if the page is scrolled, a fixed element will remain in the same position. This is useful, for example, for a fixed header or navigation bar.

A block element with a `position` of `static` or `relative` will, by default, take up the full width of its container. However, if an element is given a `position` of `absolute` or `fixed`, this will no longer be the case. It will only be as wide as it needs to be to fit its content. This can usually be solved by adding a `width: 100%` to the element if the full width behavior is still desired.

position: sticky

A `sticky` element is a combination of `relative` and `fixed`. The element acts as a relatively positioned element, scrolling with the document. When the element reaches a specified point, it turns into a fixed element. This point is specified via a `top`, `right`, `bottom`, or `left` value.

Compatibility note   `position: sticky` is not supported in Internet Explorer.

---

z-index and stacking contexts

When elements have a position of fixed, absolute, or sticky, they can obscure other elements. This may not always behave the way we want. For example, suppose you have a page with a fixed header. Later, you open a modal dialog with a semitransparent overlay behind it. However, the header is not obscured by the overlay; rather, it sits on top of it.

Listing 7-12. An example of a z-index issue

```
<style>
  .header {
    background-color: red;
    color: white;
    height: 1rem;
    left: 0;
    padding: 1rem;
    position: fixed;
    top: 0;
    width: 100%;
  }

  .body {
    margin-top: 3.5rem;
  }

  .overlay {
    background-color: rgba(0, 0, 0, 0.5);
    height: 100%;
    left: 0;
    position: absolute;
    top: 0;
    width: 100%;
  }
</style>
```

```
<div class="overlay"></div>
<div class="container">
  <div class="header">Header</div>
  <div class="body">
    Some other page content
  </div>
</div>
```

Figure 7-13. *The header is above the overlay*

The main text content is covered by the overlay, but the header is not. This can be solved by giving these elements z-index values. z-index determines the stacking order of elements along the z-axis – which element is on top of which. z-index is a relative measure that can take any numeric value. Items with a higher z-index will appear on top of those with a lower one.

In Listing 7-13, we'll give the header a z-index of 100 and the overlay a z-index of 200.

Listing 7-13. Adding z-index properties

```
<style>
  .header {
    background-color: red;
    color: white;
    height: 1rem;
    left: 0;
    padding: 1rem;
    position: fixed;
    top: 0;
```

```
    width: 100%;
    z-index: 100;
  }

  .body {
    margin-top: 3.5rem;
  }

  .overlay {
    background-color: rgba(0, 0, 0, 0.5);
    height: 100%;
    left: 0;
    position: absolute;
    top: 0;
    width: 100%;
    z-index: 200;
  }
</style>

<div class="overlay"></div>
<div class="container">
  <div class="header">Header</div>
  <div class="body">
    Some other page content
  </div>
</div>
```

Figure 7-14. *The overlay now covers all content*

Because the overlay has a higher `z-index` than the header, it now appears on top of the header.

Stacking contexts

As it turns out, `z-index` doesn't control an element's z-axis ordering globally within the entire document. It only controls the `z-index` relative to other elements within a given *stacking context*.

Initially, there is one stacking context, formed by the root of the document (the `html` element). Within the document, there are certain other elements that will create a new stacking context:

- Any element that has a `position` other than `static` and a `z-index` other than `auto`

- Any element with an `opacity` less than 1

- Any element that is a child of a `flex` or `grid` container and a `z-index` other than `auto`

There are others, but these are the most common. If no `z-index` is given, there are certain stacking rules that are applied inside a stacking context. These are, from bottom to top:

- The background and borders of the element that creates the stacking context

- Descendant elements of the element that creates the stacking context that are not positioned

- Descendant elements of the element that creates the stacking context that are positioned

These rules, in conjunction with explicitly set `z-index` properties, determine the final stacking order of elements.

Let's walk through a series of examples that illustrate `z-index` and stacking contexts.

Listing 7-14. A stacking context example

```
<style>
  .container-1 {
    background-color: red;
    width: 10rem;
    height: 10rem;
    position: relative;
    z-index: 100;
  }

  .container-2 {
    background-color: blue;
    width: 10rem;
    height: 10rem;
    position: relative;
    z-index: 100;
  }

  .inner-1 {
    background-color: green;
    width: 5rem;
    height: 5rem;
    position: relative;
    top: 7.5rem;
  }

  .inner-2 {
    background-color: orange;
    width: 5rem;
    height: 5rem;
    position: relative;
    top: -2.5rem;
  }
</style>

<div class="container-1">
  <div class="inner-1"></div>
```

```
</div>
<div class="container-2">
  <div class="inner-2"></div>
</div>
```

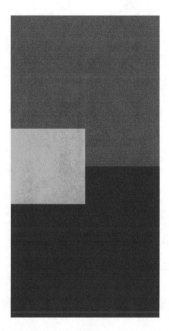

Figure 7-15. *The rendered result*

Note that the two container elements both have position set to relative and a z-index of 100. This means that each of these elements creates a new stacking context.

The two inner boxes – the green one and the orange one – have been positioned so that they are on top of each other. The orange one is on top. We can't see the green one because it's directly underneath. Figure 7-16 shows a cross-section view of the elements (dotted lines indicate stacking contexts):

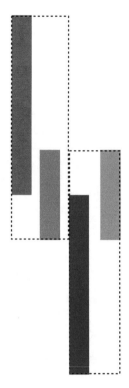

Figure 7-16. *A cross-section view*

Suppose we want the green box to be on top. We can try adjusting the green box's
z-index to be 200, which is higher than all the others. Unfortunately, we get the same
result as is shown in Figure 7-15. However, the cross-section has changed slightly, as is
shown in Figure 7-17.

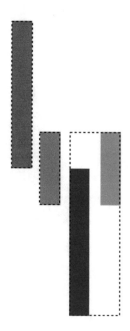

Figure 7-17. *The changed cross-section*

By setting the z-index property on the relatively positioned green box, we've created a new stacking context rooted at the green box. To demonstrate this further, let's try changing the z-index of the green box to 50.

The result, and the cross-section, are the same as before. Even though the green box has a lower z-index (50) than the red box (100), it's in a higher stacking context, so it will still appear above the red box.

As you can see, z-index issues can be difficult to debug. Understanding how stacking contexts work is critical to solving these issues.

Floats

You can use the float property to make an element "float" to the left or the right and text and other inline elements will flow around it.

Listing 7-15. A basic float

```
<style>
  .container {
    width: 10rem;
  }

  .floating {
    background-color: red;
    float: right;
    height: 3rem;
    width: 3rem;
  }
</style>

<div class="container">
  <div class="floating"></div>
  Lorem ipsum dolor sit amet, consectetur adipiscing elit. Donec nec sapien
  dolor. Nunc condimentum sem nec commodo sollicitudin.
</div>
```

Lorem ipsum dolor sit amet, consectetur adipiscing elit. Donec nec sapien dolor. Nunc condimentum sem nec commodo sollicitudin.

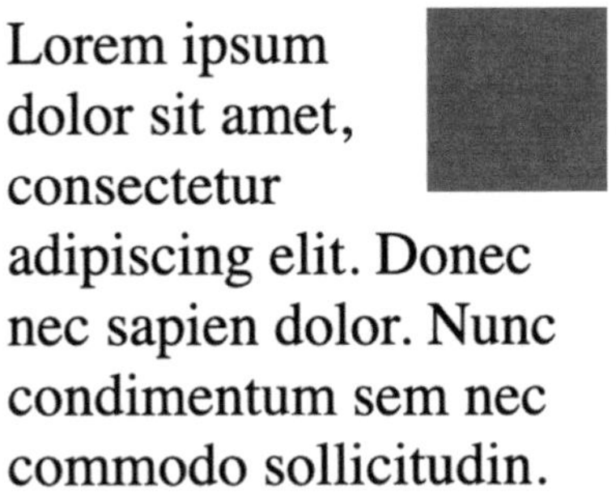

Figure 7-18. *The floated red box*

The red box is floated to the right, and the text flows around it. The float property can be set to left or right, or if you need to take text direction into account (left-to-right vs. right-to-left languages), you can use the more generic inline-start or inline-end.

When the float property is applied to an element, it is removed from the flow of the document. It then "floats" to the left or right, stopping when it reaches the edge of the containing element, or another floated element. In Figure 7-18, the red box moved to the edge of the container. Here's another example with two floated elements.

Listing 7-16. Two floating elements

```
<style>
  .container {
    width: 10rem;
  }

  .floating,
  .floating-2 {
    float: right;
    height: 3rem;
    width: 3rem;
  }

  .floating {
    background-color: red;
  }

  .floating-2 {
    background-color: blue;
  }
</style>

<div class="container">
  <div class="floating"></div>
  <div class="floating-2"></div>
  Lorem ipsum dolor sit amet, consectetur adipiscing elit. Donec nec sapien
  dolor. Nunc condimentum sem nec commodo sollicitudin.
</div>
```

Lorem ipsum dolor sit amet, consectetur adipiscing elit. Donec nec sapien dolor. Nunc condimentum sem nec commodo sollicitudin.

Figure 7-19. *The two floating boxes*

First, the red box is floated right, to the edge of the container. Next, the blue box is floated right, to the edge of the red box.

Clearing floats

The clear property can be used on an element to indicate that it can't be alongside a floated element in a given direction. The clear property can be none (the default), left, right, both, inline-start, or inline-end. If an element is cleared in a given direction, and there is a floated element there, the element will be moved so that it is below the floated element. Consider Listing 7-17, where there is a floated element on each side. We use clear: right on the content.

Listing 7-17. Clearing floats

```
<style>
  .container {
    width: 10rem;
  }

  .floating {
    background-color: red;
    float: right;
    height: 3rem;
    width: 3rem;
  }
```

```
  .floating-2 {
    background-color: blue;
    float: left;
    height: 5rem;
    width: 3rem;
  }

  .content {
    clear: right;
  }
</style>

<div class="container">
  <div class="floating"></div>
  <div class="floating-2"></div>
  <div class="content">
    Lorem ipsum dolor sit amet, consectetur adipiscing elit. Donec nec sapien
    dolor. Nunc condimentum sem nec commodo sollicitudin.
  </div>
</div>
```

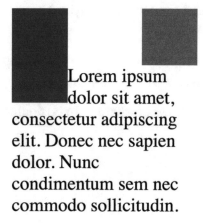

Figure 7-20. *The rendered result*

The content has been moved to below the right-floated red box. Since the blue box on the left is taller, it is allowed to be floated alongside the content.

Summary

In this chapter, we looked at basic CSS layout and positioning:

- Padding is the spacing between an element's content and its border.

- Margin is the spacing between an element's border and other elements.

- An element is said to be positioned if it has a `position` other than `static`.

- Elements can have a `position` value of `static`, `relative`, `absolute`, `fixed`, or `sticky`:

  - Statically positioned elements flow normally.

  - Relatively positioned elements are positioned relative to their normal position in the document.

  - Absolutely positioned elements are positioned relative to their nearest positioned ancestor.

  - Fixed-positioned elements remain fixed to the viewport.

  - Sticky-positioned elements are a hybrid between relative and fixed position.

- The `z-index` property controls the vertical stacking order of an element within a given stacking context.

- The `float` property allows an element to be floated to the left or right sides of its container.

CHAPTER 8

Transforms

CSS transforms take an element and apply one of several possible transformation functions to it. For example, an element can be rotated in 2D or 3D space, scaled, skewed, or translated (moved). Transforms can be used to create all kinds of interesting effects on their own and become more powerful when combined with transitions and animations.

Transforms are specified with the `transform` property. Its value is one or more *transform functions*. Multiple transforms can be applied by providing a space-separated list of transform functions. The following sections will go over the most common classes of transform functions.

Perspective

The `perspective` transform activates 3D space for an element. It defines how "far away" the object is from the user, as if the screen had depth. Used by itself, the `perspective` transform has no visible effect. But when used in combination with other transforms, it can greatly affect the final result.

Rotation

The rotation functions rotate elements around a given axis. They take the angle to rotate as an argument. The angle can be whole or fractional and is given in one of several units:

- deg: Degrees. A full circle is `360deg`.

- grad: Gradians. A full circle is `400grad`.

- rad: Radians. A full circle is approximately 2π radians, or approximately `6.28rad`.

- turn: Number of turns. A full circle is `1turn`.

157

A positive angle rotates the element clockwise; a negative angle rotates it counterclockwise. Note that an element can be rotated more than one full circle.

Axis

There are three axes of rotation:

- X-axis: Goes from left to right across the page

- Y-axis: Goes from the top of the page to the bottom

- Z-axis: 3D axis, goes from the "surface" of the page out toward you

These three axes are visualized in Figure 8-1.

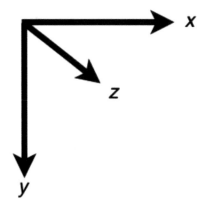

Figure 8-1. *The three axes of rotation*

Origin

A rotation also has an origin. The element is rotated around this origin point. By default, it is the center of the element, as shown in Figure 8-2.

Figure 8-2. *The default rotation origin*

However, a different origin may be specified via the transform-origin property. This will affect the final position of the element.

Figure 8-3. *A different rotation origin*

transform-origin is specified as one, two, or three values. These values correspond to the X, Y, and Z offsets of the transform origin point. These can be size values such as 10px or 25% or one of the keywords left, center, right, top, and bottom.

rotate/rotateZ

The rotate and rotateZ functions rotate an element around the Z-axis. They both have the same effect.

Listing 8-1. Rotating around the Z-axis

```
<style>
  .rotate {
    width: 10rem;
    height: 5rem;
    background: skyblue;
    margin: 5rem;
    transform: rotate(45deg);
  }
</style>

<div class="rotate">Hello World!</div>
```

Figure 8-4. *The rotated element*

rotateX

The rotateX function rotates an element around the X-axis. It is best illustrated when used in combination with the perspective transform.

Listing 8-2. Rotating around the X-axis

```
<style>
  .rotate {
    width: 10rem;
    height: 5rem;
    background: skyblue;
    margin: 5rem;
    transform: perspective(200px)
               rotateX(45deg);
  }
</style>

<div class="rotate">Hello World!</div>
```

Figure 8-5. *The rotated element*

rotateY

The rotateY function rotates an element around the y-axis.

Listing 8-3. Rotating an element around the Y-axis

```
<style>
  .rotate {
    width: 10rem;
    height: 5rem;
    background: skyblue;
    margin: 5rem;
    transform: perspective(200px)
               rotateY(45deg);
  }
</style>

<div class="rotate">Hello World!</div>
```

Figure 8-6. *The rotated element*

rotate3d

The `rotate3d` function rotates an element around an arbitrary axis in 3D space. This is done by defining a direction vector in the 3D coordinate system. The vector is defined by specifying the component of the vector in each direction as a value between 0 and 1. The element is rotated around that vector by the given angle.

Listing 8-4. Rotating an element in 3D space

```
<style>
  .rotate {
    width: 10rem;
    height: 5rem;
    background: skyblue;
    margin: 5rem;
    transform: perspective(200px)
               rotate3d(1, 1, 0, 45deg);
  }
</style>

<div class="rotate">Hello World!</div>
```

Figure 8-7. *The rotated element*

Translation

The next type of transform we'll look at is translation. Translating an element means moving it from its original position.

translate

The translate function moves an element in 2D space. It takes one or two arguments, corresponding to the X-axis and Y-axis, respectively. The flow of the document is not affected by translating an element; a blank space is left where the element's original position was.

Listing 8-5. Translating an element

```
<style>
  div {
    width: 5rem;
    height: 5rem;
    display: inline-block;
  }

  .one {
    background: orangered;
  }
```

```
  .two {
    background: rebeccapurple;
    transform: translate(2rem, 2rem);
  }

  .three {
    background: skyblue;
  }
</style>

<div class="one"></div>
<div class="two"></div>
<div class="three"></div>
```

The purple box in Figure 8-8 was translated 2rem to the left and 2rem down, but its original position leaves a "hole" in the layout. The red and blue boxes do not change their position to compensate for the translated element.

Figure 8-8. *The translated element*

The translateX and translateY functions perform translation horizontally and vertically, respectively. The effect is the same as when using the translate function. That is, translateX(1rem) is equivalent to translate(1rem, 0), and translateY(1rem) is equivalent to translate(0, 1rem).

translateZ

The translateZ function moves an element along the Z-axis. It has the effect of moving an element closer to or farther away from the user's perspective. It only has a visible effect when used in combination with the perspective function.

Listing 8-6. Translating an element along the Z-axis

```
<style>
  div {
    width: 5rem;
    height: 5rem;
    display: inline-block;
  }

  .one {
    background: orangered;
  }

  .two {
    background: rebeccapurple;
    transform: perspective(200px)
               translateZ(2rem);
  }

  .three {
    background: skyblue;
  }
</style>

<div class="one"></div>
<div class="two"></div>
<div class="three"></div>
```

In Figure 8-9, the purple box has the appearance of being moved closer to the user.

Figure 8-9. *The translated element*

translate3d

Like rotate3d, translate3d allows you to specify a vector in 3D space. The element is then translated along that vector. The three arguments define the X, Y, and Z components of the vector.

Listing 8-7. Translating an element in 3D space

```
<style>
  div {
    width: 5rem;
    height: 5rem;
    display: inline-block;
  }

  .one {
    background: orangered;
  }

  .two {
    background: rebeccapurple;
    transform: perspective(200px)
               translate3d(1rem, 2rem, 3rem);
  }

  .three {
    background: skyblue;
  }
</style>
```

```
<div class="one"></div>
<div class="two"></div>
<div class="three"></div>
```

The purple box in Figure 8-10 has been translated along all three axes.

Figure 8-10. *The translated element*

Scaling

A scaling transform function alters the size of the element, scaling its contents as it grows or shrinks. Unlike the translation functions, which take a size value, the scaling functions take multiples of the original size as arguments. For example, scale(1, 1) would perform no scaling. scale(2, 3) would scale the element to two times as large in the horizontal direction and three times as large in the vertical direction.

The arguments to scaling functions do not have to be integers. For example, values such as scale(1.25, 2.6) are also accepted.

By default, the scaling functions perform the transform starting at the center at the element. This can be changed by giving a value for the transform-origin property. Also, note that scaling an element will not cause its container to grow to fit the new size. The flow of the document is not affected.

Figure 8-11. *No scale (left), scale with origin at center (middle), and scale with origin at top (right)*

scale

The scale function scales an element along just the X, or the X and Y axes in 2D space. It takes one or two arguments. When one argument is given, it is treated as the X value, and when two arguments are given, they are treated as the X and Y values, respectively.

Listing 8-8. Scaling an element

```
<style>
  .scale {
    background: skyblue;
    text-align: center;
    transform: scale(2, 5);
    margin: 5rem auto;
    width: 10rem;
  }
</style>

<div class="scale">Hello world!</div>
```

Figure 8-12. *The scaled element*

If you only want to scale in one direction, you can also use the scaleX or scaleY functions.

scaleZ

scaleZ scales along the Z-axis. It has no noticeable effect when used alone. The effect is best seen when used in combination with perspective and another transform like rotateX.

Figure 8-13 shows an example of an element with and without the scaleZ transform.

```
transform: perspective(200px) rotateX(45deg);
```

```
transform: perspective(200px) scaleZ(5) rotateX(45deg);
```

Figure 8-13. *The effect of the scaleZ function*

scale3d

Like rotate3d and translate3d, there is also a scale3d function. As with the other related functions, scale3d scales along a vector with X, Y, and Z components. Different magnitudes can be given for the different axes, so an element can be scaled at different rates in all three directions.

Skewing

The last set of transform functions we'll look at are the skewing functions. These functions distort an element by a given angle in the X and Y directions. Like the rotation functions, the angle can be given in one of several different units.

Listing 8-9. An example of the skew function

```
<style>
  .skew {
    background: skyblue;
    transform: skew(45deg, 20deg);
    width: 10rem;
    font-size: 2rem;
    text-align: center;
    margin: 5rem;
  }
</style>

<div class="skew">Hello world!</div>
```

Figure 8-14. *The skewed element*

There are also skewX and skewY functions as well, if you only want to skew an element in one direction.

Applying multiple transforms

As we have seen already, you can apply multiple transforms to a single element. The multiple transforms are passed as a space-separated list to the transform property. One important thing to note is when an element is rotated, the axes move with the element as well. This is best illustrated with an example. Listing 8-10 has simple box, rotated 45 degrees. We'll put a container around it so we can see how it moves.

Listing 8-10. Rotating an element

```
<style>
  .container {
    border: 1px solid black;
    width: 15rem;
    height: 15rem;
    margin: 5rem;
  }

  .box {
    transform: rotate(45deg);
    background: skyblue;
    width: 10rem;
    height: 10rem;
  }
</style>

<div class="container">
  <div class="box"></div>
</div>
```

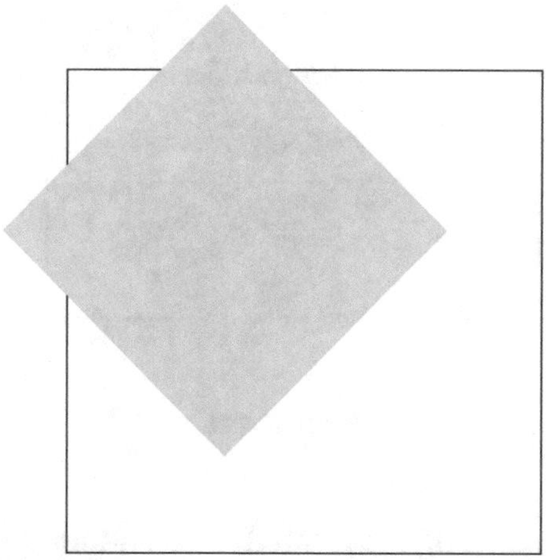

Figure 8-15. *The rotated box*

Now that we have rotated the element, the element's coordinate system has rotated as well, as shown in Figure 8-16.

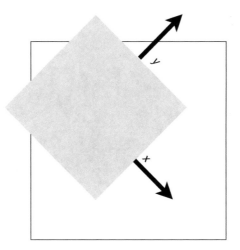

Figure 8-16. *The rotated box's coordinate system*

To illustrate this, we'll add a `translateX(100px)` to the `transform` property:

`transform: rotate(45deg) translateX(100px);`

Figure 8-17. *The element's resulting position*

Note that the box moved along the rotated X-axis rather than the page's X-axis.

With multiple CSS transforms, the order the transforms are listed in matters. If we reverse the two transforms in the preceding example, so that the `translateX` comes first, the end result looks different, as shown in Figure 8-18.

`transform: translateX(100px) rotate(45deg);`

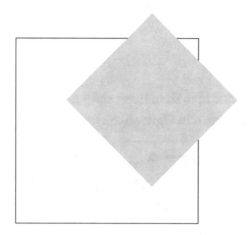

Figure 8-18. *The element's new position*

This time, the order of transformations was different. The box was first translated along the X-axis, and then it was rotated. Because the box wasn't rotated when it was translated, it moved along the page's X-axis.

You can even specify multiple transforms of the same type. Let's add another translateX transform to the previous example.

```
transform: translateX(100px)
           rotate(45deg)
           translateX(100px);
```

Figure 8-19. *Applying three transforms to the element*

We moved the element 100 pixels along the X-axis then rotated it 45 degrees, as before. When we rotated the box, its coordinate system changed. When we applied the second translateX transform, the box moved along its rotated X-axis.

Examples

Making a heart

We can utilize CSS transforms to make a heart shape. A heart is really just a rotated square with two circles, as shown in Figure 8-20.

Figure 8-20. *The component parts of the heart shape*

All we need to do is take a square, rotate it 45 degrees, and place two circles in the proper position. We can actually do this with a single div element. The div will make up the square part of the heart. We'll then use the ::before and ::after pseudo-elements to draw the circles.

Let's start with the rotated square, in Listing 8-11.

Listing 8-11. The rotated square

```
<style>
  .heart {
    border: 5px solid red;
    transform: rotate(45deg);
    width: 10rem;
    height: 10rem;
    margin: 10rem auto;
  }
</style>

<div class="heart"></div>
```

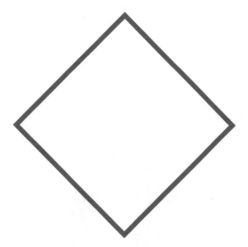

Figure 8-21. *The rotated square*

Now we need to create the two circles by adding ::before and ::after pseudo-elements, which we do in Listing 8-12. A circle can easily be created by setting a square element's border-radius property to 50%.

Listing 8-12. Adding the circles as pseudo-elements

```
<style>
  .heart {
    border: 5px solid red;
    transform: rotate(45deg);
    width: 10rem;
    height: 10rem;
    margin: 10rem auto;
  }

  .heart::after,
  .heart::before {
    border-radius: 50%;
    content: '';
    width: 10rem;
    height: 10rem;
```

```
    position: absolute;
    background: red;
  }
</style>

<div class="heart"></div>
```

Figure 8-22. *The circle pseudo-elements*

The circles are stacked on top of each other in the center of the square. Now we just need to move them out to either side. Remember that the coordinate system rotated with the square. The left-hand circle needs to be moved 5rem (half of the size of the square) to the left along the X-axis, and the right-hand circle needs to be moved 5rem higher along the Y-axis.

While we're at it, we'll fill in the square with red to complete the shape in Listing 8-13.

Listing 8-13. Completing the code for the heart

```
<style>
  .heart {
    background: red;
    transform: rotate(45deg);
    width: 10rem;
    height: 10rem;
    margin: 10rem auto;
  }
```

```
.heart::after,
.heart::before {
  border-radius: 50%;
  content: '';
  width: 10rem;
  height: 10rem;
  position: absolute;
  background: red;
}

.heart::before {
  transform: translateX(-5rem);
}

.heart::after {
  transform: translateY(-5rem);
}
</style>

<div class="heart"></div>
```

Figure 8-23. *The completed heart*

Making a cube

Now let's build something three-dimensional. A cube is a simple enough shape to make. There will be a container element for the cube, the cube itself, and one element for each of the six faces of the cube. Listing 8-14 has the initial markup and CSS.

Listing 8-14. The initial cube code

```
<style>
  .container {
    width: 10rem;
    height: 10rem;
    perspective: 500px;
    margin: 5rem;
  }

  .cube {
    position: relative;
    width: 10rem;
    height: 10rem;
    transform-style: preserve-3d;
    transform: rotate3d(1, 1, 0, 45deg);
  }

  .face {
    width: 10rem;
    height: 10rem;
    background: skyblue;
    border: 2px solid black;
    position: absolute;
    opacity: 0.5;
    text-align: center;
  }
</style>

<div class="container">
  <div class="cube">
    <div class="face top">Top</div>
```

```
    <div class="face bottom">Bottom</div>
    <div class="face left">Left</div>
    <div class="face right">Right</div>
    <div class="face front">Front</div>
    <div class="face back">Back</div>
  </div>
</div>
```

We've seen everything here except for the transform-style property. By default, an element's children are flattened to be on the same plane. This means they are "squashed" down to 2D space. We want to make a 3D cube, so that won't work here. Setting transform-style to preserve-3d will allow the cube's child elements to exist in 3D space.

Compatibility note   transform-style: preserve-3d is not supported in Internet Explorer.

Currently, all of the faces of the cube are lying flat, stacked on top of one another since they are absolutely positioned. What we need to do is rotate the faces, in 3D space, so that they are facing the correct way, then move them out from the center to form the cube.

It's a little difficult to see what's going on when we're looking head on at the cube, so we've rotated the cube element to see it at a 45-degree angle, which will let us better see its 3D structure. We've also set the opacity to 0.5 to help visualize the cube.

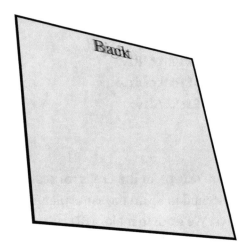

Figure 8-24. *The cube faces all stacked on top of each other*

Now we need to rotate the faces to their proper orientations. The front doesn't need to be rotated, as it's already facing forward. We need to rotate the back around the Y-axis by 180 degrees, the left and right around the Y-axis by 90 degrees (-90 and 90 respectively), and the top and bottom around the X-axis by 90 degrees (-90 and 90 respectively). Let's do this in Listing 8-15.

Listing 8-15. Rotating the cube faces

```
<style>
  .container {
    width: 10rem;
    height: 10rem;
    perspective: 500px;
    margin: 5rem;
  }

  .cube {
    position: relative;
    width: 10rem;
    height: 10rem;
    transform-style: preserve-3d;
    transform: rotate3d(1, 1, 0, 45deg);
  }
```

```
.face {
  width: 10rem;
  height: 10rem;
  background: skyblue;
  border: 2px solid black;
  position: absolute;
  opacity: 0.5;
  text-align: center;
}

.back { transform: rotateY(180deg); }
.left { transform: rotateY(-90deg); }
.right { transform: rotateY(90deg); }
.top { transform: rotateX(90deg); }
.bottom { transform: rotateX(-90deg); }

</style>

<div class="container">
  <div class="cube">
    <div class="face top">Top</div>
    <div class="face bottom">Bottom</div>
    <div class="face left">Left</div>
    <div class="face right">Right</div>
    <div class="face front">Front</div>
    <div class="face back">Back</div>
  </div>
</div>
```

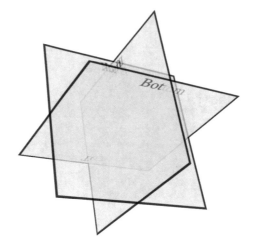

Figure 8-25. *The rotated cube faces*

Now all the faces are rotated properly, but they are still at the center of the cube. Since the cube's size is 10rem, and the faces are in the middle, each face must be moved out by 5rem in the proper direction: the front and back along the Z-axis, the left and right along the X-axis, and the top and bottom along the Y-axis.

Listing 8-16. The final cube code

```
<style>
  .container {
    width: 10rem;
    height: 10rem;
    perspective: 500px;
    margin: 5rem;
  }

  .cube {
    position: relative;
    width: 10rem;
    height: 10rem;
    transform-style: preserve-3d;
    transform: rotate3d(1, 1, 0, 45deg);
  }
```

```
.face {
  width: 10rem;
  height: 10rem;
  background: skyblue;
  border: 2px solid black;
  position: absolute;
  opacity: 0.5;
  text-align: center;
}

.front {
  transform: translateZ(5rem);
}

.back {
  transform: translateZ(-5rem) rotateY(180deg);
}
.left {
  transform: translateX(-5rem) rotateY(-90deg);
}
.right {
  transform: translateX(5rem) rotateY(90deg);
}
.top {
  transform: translateY(-5rem) rotateX(90deg);
}
.bottom {
  transform: translateY(5rem) rotateX(-90deg);
}
</style>

<div class="container">
  <div class="cube">
    <div class="face top">Top</div>
    <div class="face bottom">Bottom</div>
    <div class="face left">Left</div>
    <div class="face right">Right</div>
```

```
    <div class="face front">Front</div>
    <div class="face back">Back</div>
  </div>
</div>
```

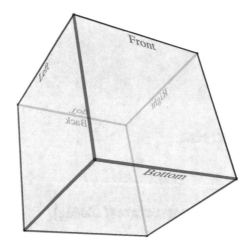

Figure 8-26. *The completed cube*

Summary

In this chapter, we learned about the CSS transform types:

- Rotation

- Translation

- Scaling

- Skewing

We also learned about concepts such as perspective, axes, transform origins, and 3D transformation vectors. Lastly, we saw a few practical examples of making shapes with CSS transforms.

CHAPTER 9

Transitions and Animations

CSS transforms are useful on their own, but they are even more powerful when used in combination with transitions and animations.

Transitions

A CSS transition is a way of animating an element from one state to another. They are similar to, but not quite the same as, CSS animations.

During the lifetime of a page, an element's CSS properties can change. For example, the user could hover over an element, triggering the :hover pseudo-class, which could apply some different styling. Or, maybe, a class is added to or removed from an element with JavaScript. In both of these cases, any style changes are applied immediately.

Let's take the example of a hover state. Suppose we have the styles for a button shown in Listing 9-1.

Listing 9-1. Some button styles

```
button.fancy-button {
  background: blue;
}

button.fancy-button:hover {
  background: red;
  transform: scale(1.1);
}
```

© Joe Attardi 2020
J. Attardi, *Modern CSS*, https://doi.org/10.1007/978-1-4842-6294-8_9

When the user hovers over a fancy button with their mouse, two things will happen. The background color will immediately change from blue to red, and the button will immediately snap to a scale factor of 1.1. This can be visually jarring. We can improve this experience with CSS transitions.

It's easy to add transitions with the `transition` property, as shown in Listing 9-2.

Listing 9-2. Adding a transition

```
button.fancy-button {
  background: blue;
  transition: 500ms;
}

button.fancy-button:hover {
  background: red;
  transform: scale(1.1);
}
```

Now, when the user hovers the mouse over a fancy button, it will behave differently. Instead of immediately snapping to the new background color and size, the element will gradually *transition* to the new color and scale over a period of 500 milliseconds. You can think of these two states (blue background/scale 1, red background/scale 1.1) as *keyframes* in an animation. You don't have to define all the states in between the two keyframes – the browser will animate the transition between the two states.

The color will gradually change from blue to shades of purple to the final color of red. At the same time, the size will animate from `scale(1)` to `scale(1.1)`, making the element appear to grow over the course of the 500 milliseconds.

This is the simplest possible transition. All properties on the element that support animations/transitions – and not all properties do; see `https://developer.mozilla.org/en-US/docs/Web/CSS/CSS_animated_properties` for an exhaustive list – will be transitioned to their new values over 500 milliseconds.

We can also have multistage transitions. For example, we could have the background color transition first, and then only after the color change is complete, we could then transition the scale transform.

The `transition` property takes a comma-separated list of transitions. When only a duration is given, like the given example, the transition property defaults to `all`.

However, we can specify individual properties we want to transition along with a duration, and a delay. For this example, we want the following two transition stages:

- Transition the color over 500 milliseconds.

- Transform the scale over 500 milliseconds, with a 500-millisecond delay.

This will yield a total transition time of 1 second.

Listing 9-3. A multistage transition

```
button.fancy-button {
  background: blue;
  transition: background-color 500ms,
              transform 500ms 500ms;
}

button.fancy-button:hover {
  background: red;
  transform: scale(1.1);
}
```

When specifying a transition in this way, the first argument is the name of the property, the second argument is the duration, and the third argument is the delay. Now, when we hover over the button, the color transitions from blue to red, while the scale remains unchanged. Once the color has transitioned after 500 milliseconds, then the scale transition begins, which lasts another 500 milliseconds.

The transition property is a shorthand property like border or background. The transition property earlier is actually shorthand for the following properties shown in Listing 9-4.

Listing 9-4. Using the separate transition-related properties

```
button.fancy-button {
  background: blue;
  transition-property: background-color, transform;
  transition-duration: 500ms, 500ms;
  transition-delay: 0ms, 500ms;
}
```

```
button.fancy-button:hover {
  background: red;
  transform: scale(1.1);
}
```

Time units

The timing for transitions (and animations, as we'll see later) can be specified in either seconds (s) or milliseconds (ms). Fractional values can be used; that is, 500 milliseconds can be specified as 500ms or 0.5s.

Easing functions

If you tried the given example, you may have noticed that the transition does not happen at a linear rate. That is, it appears to start out slow, speed up in the middle, then slow down again at the end. This is the default transition timing function, which is called ease. There are other built-in timing functions as well. Formally, these are specified as easing functions. These functions are visualized by plotting a graph, with the time on the X-axis and the animation progress on the Y-axis.

These functions are usually given as *Cubic Bezier* curves. A Cubic Bezier curve is created by specifying four points on a graph. The points are plotted, and a curve is drawn. A good way to think of how the curve is drawn is like this: Think of a straight line drawn between the first and last points. Then, the second and third points "bend" the line up and down toward them to make a curve.

In a Cubic Bezier curve for a CSS easing function, the first point is always (0, 0) and represents the start state of the animation or transition. The last point is always (1, 1) and represents the end state. The X-coordinate of the two middle points must be between 0 and 1, or else it is not considered a valid easing function and will be ignored.

Since the first and last points of the curve are always (0, 0) and (1, 1), we only need to specify the X and Y coordinates of the two middle points that "bend" the curve:

```
transition-timing-function:
  cubic-bezier(.17, .67, .9, .6);
```

The given cubic-bezier function yields the curve shown in Figure 9-1.

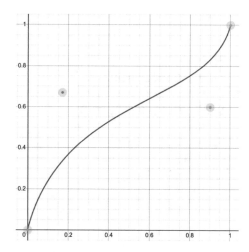

Figure 9-1. *The plotted Bezier curve*

There are several built-in easing functions which you can specify by name instead of a cubic-bezier function. These functions are shown in Table 9-1 with Figures 9-2 through 9-6.

Table 9-1. *Built-in easing functions*

Function	Equivalent cubic-bezier values	Graph
linear	0.0, 0.0, 1.0, 1.0	

(continued)

Table 9-1. (*continued*)

Function	Equivalent cubic-bezier values	Graph
ease	0.25, 0.1, 0.25, 1.0	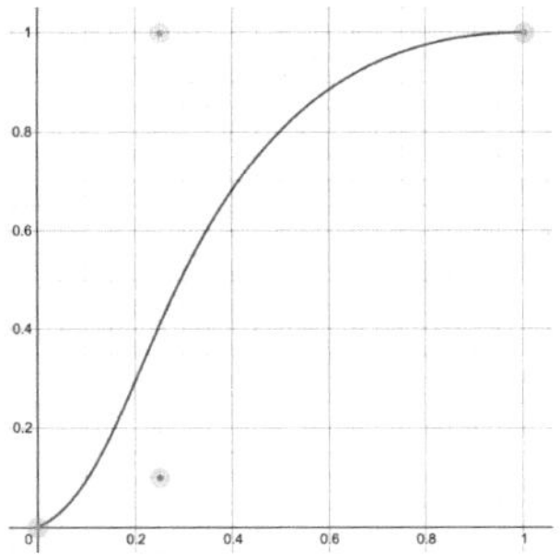
ease-in	0.42, 0.0, 1.0, 1.0	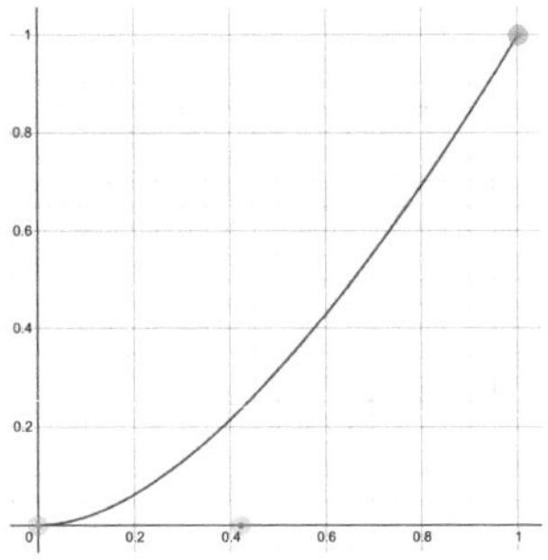
ease-out	0.0, 0.0, 0.58, 1.0	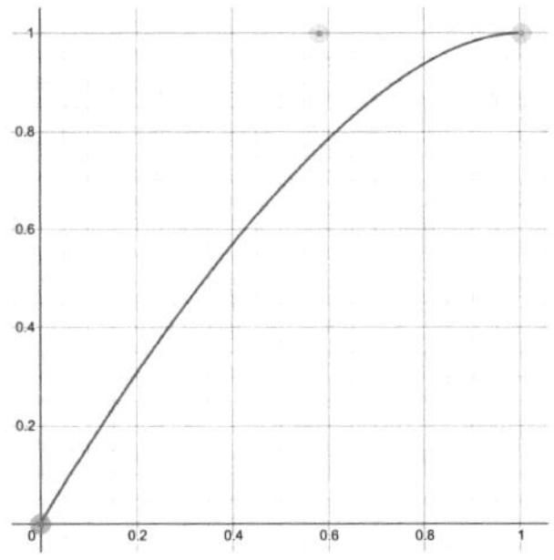
ease-in-out	0.42, 0.0, 0.58, 1.0	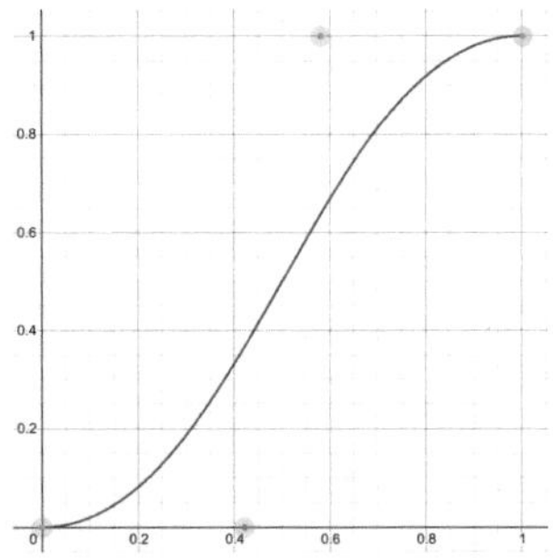

The animation progress (the Y-axis) can also bend above 1 or below 0 to create a "bouncing" effect for some properties. For example, the easing function cubic-bezier(0.680, -0.550, 0.265, 1.550) results in the graph shown in Figure 9-7.

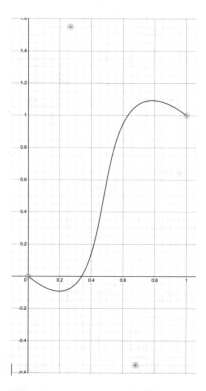

Figure 9-7. *An easing function with a "bounce" effect*

Notice how the high and low points cause the curve to bend above 1 and below 0. This means, for the earlier example, that the scale transform would drop below 1 (the initial value) and go above 1.1 (the end value).

It can be difficult to craft these functions by hand, so there are several great resources online to help you design custom ones:

- Ceaser by Matthew Lein

    https://matthewlein.com/tools/ceaser

- cubic-bezier.com by Lea Verou

    https://cubic-bezier.com

Easing functions can also be specified as *step functions*. A step function divides the transition into equally sized steps in a given direction. Instead of a smooth transition like with a Bezier curve, they jump from step to step, skipping the intermediate states.

These are specified as `steps(step-count, direction)`. `step-count` is a number indicating the number of these steps, and `direction` is one of the following values:

- `jump-start`, `start`: The change in state happens at the beginning of each step, beginning with the start of the transition. Because the first "jump" happens immediately, the initial state of the transition is effectively lost.

- `jump-end`, `end`: The change in state happens at the end of each step, ending with the end of the transition. With this value, the end state of the transition is lost.

- `jump-none`: With this value, the start and end state of the transition are both preserved. The first step is the initial state, and the last step is the end state.

- `jump-both`: With this value, the start and end state of the transition are both lost.

Compatibility note   The jump- keywords are not supported in Internet Explorer 11. Also, at the time of writing, they are not supported in Safari.

CSS transitions can be a powerful tool to add better interactivity to a website or app. However, they are limited in transitioning from one initial state to one final state. With CSS animations, which we'll look at next, we can have an arbitrary number of states to create even more stunning effects.

Animations

Where CSS transitions provide an animated transition from a start state to an end state, animations provide animated transitions between any arbitrary number of states.

Like transitions, animations are specified by the properties that change. Instead of being specified in a property like `transition`, they are specified in special at-rules:

@keyframes. The @keyframes rule defines the various CSS properties to be applied at given steps during the animation, and the browser will automatically animate between these states.

A @keyframes rule is given an identifier and contains two or more blocks of CSS properties. Each block is labeled with a percentage representing a fraction of the total animation duration. In the example from Listing 9-5, the element's background color will change from red to blue to green.

Listing 9-5. A basic CSS animation

```
@keyframes colors {
  0% {
    background: red;
  }

  50% {
    background: blue;
  }

  100% {
    background: green;
  }
}
```

Here, we are defining a @keyframes rule named colors. The initial state of an element using this animation will have a background color of red. At the halfway point of the animation, it will have a color of blue. Finally, at the end state, it will have a color of green. Like with transitions, the browser will automatically calculate all the intermediate colors for the animation.

0% can be replaced with the keyword from, and 100% can be replaced with the keyword to, but this is optional and has the same meaning.

Once an animation is defined in a @keyframes rule, we have to use it with an element. The @keyframes rule is referenced in the animation property of a regular CSS rule.

Listing 9-6. Applying the animation to an element

```
<style>
  @keyframes colors {
    0% {
      background: red;
    }

    50% {
      background: blue;
    }

    100% {
      background: green;
    }
  }

  .box {
    animation: colors 2s;
    width: 10rem;
    height: 10rem;
  }
</style>

<div class="box"></div>
```

The `animation` property can take many forms, as it is a shorthand for several animation-related properties. Here are some examples:

- `animation: color 2s ease-in-out 2s both`

- `animation: pulse 2s linear infinite`

When using the shorthand `animation` property, you can specify the values in almost any order, and the browser will figure out which argument means what. The one exception to this is the duration and delay. The *first* time value encountered is treated as the duration, and the *second* is treated as the delay.

Animation properties

As mentioned earlier, the animation property is a shorthand for specifying multiple animation-related properties. Here are some of the more commonly used ones.

animation-name

The identifier of the @keyframes rule that defines the animation that should be performed on the element.

animation-duration

The total duration of the animation. Can be specified in seconds (s) or milliseconds (ms).

animation-timing-function

The easing function to use for the animation.

animation-delay

By default, the animation will start immediately. Specifying an animation-delay will delay the start of the animation by the time given. Can be specified in seconds or milliseconds.

A negative value can be given for animation-delay. If a negative time value is given, the animation will start immediately at the given point of elapsed time. For example, if an animation has a duration of 1s, and the delay is given as -500ms, the animation will start immediately at the 500ms mark.

animation-fill-mode

If you try the example in Listing 9-6, you will observe some interesting behavior. The element cycles through the colors, from red to blue to green over 2 seconds, then it disappears. This is because, by default, the properties applied during the animation are no longer applied once the animation ends, and we didn't define a background color in the rule for the element. It reverts back to whatever properties were defined on the element. If the .box CSS rule had a background-color of yellow, it would run the animation then turn yellow.

Like most things in CSS, this can be changed with a property. The `animation-fill-mode` property defines how properties from the keyframes are applied to an element before the animation starts or after the animation ends (or both).

Consider the example in Listing 9-7.

Listing 9-7. An example animation

```
<style>
  @keyframes color {
    from {
      background: red;
    }

    to {
      background: blue;
    }
  }

  .animate {
    background: yellow;
    animation: color 2s;
    animation-delay: 2s;
    width: 10rem;
    height: 10rem;
  }
</style>

<div class="animate"></div>
```

We have a box that is yellow. It animates its background color starting from red, transitioning to blue. The animation happens over the course of two seconds, and there is a 2-second delay before it starts. Let's examine the different values that `animation-fill-mode` accepts and what effect they will have on this element's animation.

none

The element is yellow for 2 seconds. It then immediately switches to red, and over the next 2 seconds, it transitions to blue. After the animation completes, the background color immediately switches back to yellow. With none, the styles in the keyframes are only applied for the duration of the animation. This is the default behavior.

forwards

The element is yellow for 2 seconds. It then immediately switches to red, and the animation runs over the next 2 seconds, transitioning to blue. After the animation completes, the background color stays blue. With forwards, the styles from the last keyframe of the animation remain applied to the element after the animation ends.

backwards

The element immediately becomes red, which it remains for the next 2 seconds. Then the animation runs for 2 seconds, transitioning to blue. Once the animation is done, the background color immediately switches back to yellow. With backwards, the styles from the first keyframe are applied during the animation delay period.

both

The element immediately becomes red for 2 seconds. Then the animation runs for 2 seconds, transitioning to blue. Once the animation is done, the element remains blue. With both, you get the effects of forwards and backwards.

animation-iteration-count

By default, an animation runs only once. You can have the animation run several times by giving a number for animation-iteration-count, or you can have it loop forever by specifying the keyword infinite. Interestingly, this value does not have to be a whole number. For example, you can specify animation-iteration-count: 0.5, and the animation will play once to the halfway point only.

animation-direction

Defines whether the animation should run forward (the normal keyword) or backward (the reverse keyword). Other accepted values are alternate (runs the animation forward, then backward) and alternate-reverse (runs the animation backward, then forward).

animation-play-state

Defines whether or not the animation is currently playing. This could be manipulated with JavaScript to pause and resume an animation, for example. Accepted values are running and paused. When the animation is changed from running to paused, and later changed back to running, the animation will continue from where it left off – it won't start over from the beginning.

Multiple animations

An element can have multiple animations applied to it. The animation shorthand property, as well as all the other animation properties, supports a comma-separated list of multiple values.

Listing 9-8. Applying multiple animations to an element

```
<style>
  @keyframes color {
    from {
      background-color: red;
    }
    to {
      background-color: blue;
    }
  }

  @keyframes spin {
    from {
      transform: rotate(0);
    }
    to {
      transform: rotate(360deg);
    }
  }

  .animate {
    width: 10rem;
```

```
    height: 10rem;
    animation: color 5s alternate infinite,
               spin 1s linear infinite;
  }
</style>

<div class="animate"></div>
```

This element's color will cycle infinitely between blue and red every 5 seconds, while spinning at a rate of one rotation per 1 second, at the same time.

Figure 9-8. *The multiple animations being applied*

Performance implications

Transitions and animations are powerful. But with great power comes great responsibility. Overusing them, or using them for certain expensive properties, can result in poor performance of your page.

Property types

There are a few different categories we can put CSS properties into: layout, paint, and composite properties.

Layout properties

Layout properties are properties that affect how an element (and its surrounding content) is laid out on the page. This category includes properties like width, height, padding, and margin. These are generally the most expensive to animate.

If you animate the margin of an element, for every frame of the animation, the size taken up by the element changes. This will affect the layout of surrounding elements.

When those elements' layouts are adjusted, that could trigger even more elements to recalculate their layout. This chain reaction is known as layout thrashing and can be very costly for performance.

Paint properties

Paint properties affect how an element is painted on the screen, such as `color` or `background-image`. These properties don't affect layout, so they aren't as expensive as layout properties. However, if overused, they can still cause performance issues, particularly on mobile devices.

Composite properties

Composite properties are properties such as `transform` and `opacity`. These properties don't affect layout and are much cheaper than the other property types. Additionally, the computer's GPU can also assist with these animations, which takes a load off the CPU and makes the animations smoother.

If you're interested in CSS performance, a good site to check out is `https://csstriggers.com`. This site catalogs commonly used CSS properties and shows which ones trigger layout, paint, or composite operations.

Figure 9-9. *A screenshot of the CSS Triggers site*

The `will-change` property

Animations can sometimes be improved by setting the `will-change` property on an element. This is a hint to the browser that a certain property or properties will be changing due to an animation or transition.

Listing 9-9. Example usage of the `will-change` property

```
.my-element {
  will-change: transform, opacity;
}
```

This example provides a hint that the `transform` and `opacity` properties will be changing, so the browser can take that into account when optimizing for the animation.

However, this property should be used sparingly. The browser already does a good job optimizing layout, painting, and composite operations to help keep your animations and transitions smooth. Overusing `will-change` can interfere with that optimization and could actually make performance worse. It's intended more as a last resort to improve performance.

Compatibility note   The `will-change` property is not supported in Internet Explorer.

Avoid simultaneous animations

Try to limit the number of animations running simultaneously. Even performant animations can cause performance issues when combined with several others at once, particularly if one or more of them already have performance issues, such as animating a layout property.

When you do perform multiple animations at once, it can be useful to test each in isolation to get an idea of which ones will contribute to the most performance problems.

Accessibility

Some users may have vestibular or seizure disorders that can be triggered by rapidly moving or flashing elements in your pages. You should be mindful of this when designing your animations. Most modern operating systems allow users to disable, or reduce, animations to help alleviate this.

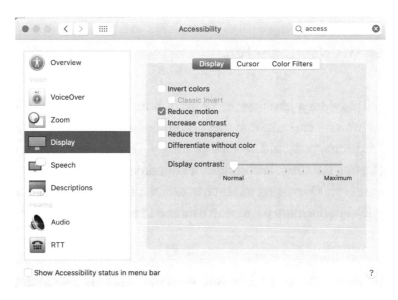

Figure 9-10. *The accessibility options in macOS*

This setting, by default, will not be honored by the HTML and CSS content of your site. Even if a user has disabled animations, your CSS animations and transitions will still run.

You can, and should, detect this scenario by using the `prefers-reduced-motion` *media query* and adjusting (or disabling) your animations accordingly. We'll get more into media queries in Chapter 11, but here's how we use it.

Listing 9-10 has a very basic loading spinner.

Listing 9-10. A spinning element

```
<style>
  @keyframes spin {
    from {
      transform: rotate(0deg);
    }
```

```
    to {
      transform: rotate(360deg);
    }
  }

  .loader {
    width: 10rem;
    height: 10rem;
    background: skyblue;
    animation: spin 500ms linear infinite;
  }
</style>

<div class="loader"></div>
```

This results in a square that spins very quickly, making one full rotation every 500ms. This could trigger seizures or other issues, as it moves very fast. We can conditionally disable the animation by using the prefers-reduced-motion media query.

Listing 9-11. The prefers-reduced-motion media query

```
@media (prefers-reduced-motion: reduce) {
  .loader {
    animation: none;
  }
}
```

When this page is loaded on a system where the user has disabled motion, the box will not be animated.

The prefers-reduced-motion query has two supported values: reduce and no-preference.

Compatibility note The prefers-reduced-motion media query is not supported in Internet Explorer.

Summary

In this chapter, we learned about CSS transitions and animations. Some key things to remember are

- A transition is used to animate an element between two states, while an animation can use any number of states.

- An easing function determines the timing of the animation progress:

  - There are several built-in easing functions: `linear`, `ease`, `ease-in`, `ease-out`, and `ease-in-out`.

- Transitions and animations have a duration, and an optional delay.

- Animations have the `animation-fill-mode` property, which determines how styles are applied before and after the animation is performed.

- Try to avoid animating layout properties, as these can negatively affect performance.

- Use the `prefers-reduced-motion` media query to improve the accessibility of your site.

CHAPTER 10

Flexbox

The Flexible Box Layout Module, more commonly known as *flexbox*, is a powerful tool for building layouts with CSS. It is not quite as powerful as CSS Grid, which we'll look at in Chapter 12, but it can solve many layout problems. Flexbox is a one-dimensional layout that can lay out elements either horizontally or vertically (but not both). An element using flexbox as its layout is referred to as a *flex container*, and the elements inside it are *flex items*.

Basic concepts

Let's go over the basic concepts to understand flexbox.

Direction

A flex container has a *direction*, defined by the flex-direction property. It can be either a row (horizontal) or column (vertical). This is shown in Figure 10-1. There are actually four values for the flex-direction property: row, row-reverse, column, and column-reverse. The meaning of row/column and row-reverse/column-reverse depends on whether the system is using a left-to-right (LTR) language or a right-to-left (RTL) language. The following sections assume an LTR language; for an RTL language, they are reversed.

A flex container is created by setting an element's display property to the value flex. This will create a block flex container. You can also create an inline flex container by setting display to inline-flex.

© Joe Attardi 2020
J. Attardi, *Modern CSS*, https://doi.org/10.1007/978-1-4842-6294-8_10

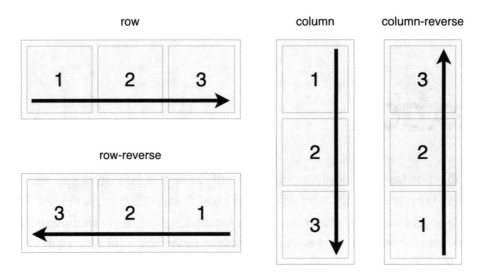

Figure 10-1. *The different values for* `flex-direction`

Axis

Related to the direction is the concept of the *axis*. The *main axis* points along the direction specified in `flex-direction`, and the *cross axis* points perpendicular to it. For example, if `flex-direction` is set to `row`, the main axis goes horizontally from left to right, and the cross axis goes vertically from top to bottom. The two flex axes are shown in Figure 10.2.

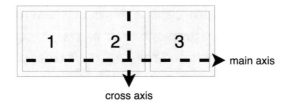

Figure 10-2. *The main axis and cross axis*

A basic flex layout

A basic flex layout is achieved by setting the container's `display` property to `flex` and setting a `flex-direction`, as demonstrated in Listing 10-1.

Listing 10-1. A basic flex layout

```
<style>
  .container {
    display: flex;
    flex-direction: row;
    border: 1px solid black;
  }

  .item,
  .item2,
  .item3 {
    background: rebeccapurple;
    font-size: 3rem;
    padding: 2rem;
    color: white;
  }

  .item2 {
    background: skyblue;
  }

  .item3 {
    background: orangered;
  }
</style>

<div class="container">
  <div class="item">1</div>
  <div class="item2">2</div>
  <div class="item3">3</div>
</div>
```

The rendered layout is shown in Figure 10-3.

Figure 10-3. *The rendered flex layout*

We can observe a few things here. First, the height of the container is just enough to fit its content. We can also see that the items are right up against each other – the flex container does not add any gap between its items. There is actually a gap property that will make the flex container set a gap between its items, but it does not have wide browser support yet.

Normally, a block element would start on a new line. But inside a flex container, this doesn't happen. The items are instead laid out along the main axis.

Sizing

What happens if the flex items don't fit within the flex container? To better see the boundaries of the container in the next example, we'll add some padding to it, as shown in Listing 10-2.

Listing 10-2. A flex container that is not wide enough to fit its items

```
<style>
  .container {
    border: 1px solid black;
    padding: 0.5rem;
    width: 500px;
    display: flex;
    flex-direction: row;
  }

  .item {
    width: 300px;
    text-align: center;
    color: white;
    font-size: 2rem;
  }
```

```
  .one {
    background: blue;
  }

  .two {
    background: red;
  }

  .three {
    background: green;
  }
</style>

<div class="container">
  <div class="item one">1</div>
  <div class="item two">2</div>
  <div class="item three">3</div>
</div>
```

The preceding code results in the layout shown in Figure 10-4.

Figure 10-4. *The rendered result*

The container only has a width of 500px and contains three items, each with a width of 300px. Yet, the items fit neatly inside the container and don't overflow. In cases like this, the browser will try to shrink flex items to fit the container.

Sometimes, the elements can be shrunk down as small as possible but still not fit within the container. When this happens, the items then will overflow the container. This is demonstrated in Listing 10-3.

Listing 10-3. Items that cannot be shrunk to fit inside the flex container

```
<style>
  .container {
    border: 1px solid black;
    padding: 0.5rem;
    width: 120px;
    display: flex;
    flex-direction: row;
  }

  .item {
    width: 300px;
    text-align: center;
    color: white;
    font-size: 2rem;
  }

  .one {
    background: blue;
  }

  .two {
    background: red;
  }

  .three {
    background: green;
  }
</style>

<div class="container">
  <div class="item one">Item 1</div>
  <div class="item two">Item 2</div>
  <div class="item three">Item 3</div>
</div>
```

This results in the layout shown in Figure 10-5, where the contents overflow the container.

Figure 10-5. The items overflow the container

Properties

There are several properties that affect flex item sizing. Some of these properties are set on the flex container, and others are set on the flex items.

flex-wrap (container)

One possible solution to the preceding problem is to use the flex-wrap property. When flex-wrap is set to wrap on the flex container, its flex items will wrap to the next line. Listing 10-4 has an example of setting a container's flex-wrap to wrap.

Listing 10-4. The flex-wrap property

```
<style>
  .container {
    border: 1px solid black;
    padding: 0.5rem;
    width: 120px;
    display: flex;
    flex-direction: row;
    flex-wrap: wrap;
  }

  .item {
    width: 300px;
    text-align: center;
    color: white;
    font-size: 2rem;
  }
```

```
  .one {
    background: blue;
  }

  .two {
    background: red;
  }

  .three {
    background: green;
  }
</style>

<div class="container">
  <div class="item one">Item 1</div>
  <div class="item two">Item 2</div>
  <div class="item three">Item 3</div>
</div>
```

This results in the flex items wrapping to the next line, as shown in Figure 10-6.

Figure 10-6. *The flex items wrap to the next line*

flex-grow (item)

By default, if the items are not large enough to fill the container, there will be empty space. An example of this is in Listing 10-5.

Listing 10-5. Empty space in the container

```
<style>
  .container {
    border: 1px solid black;
    padding: 0.5rem;
    width: 500px;
    display: flex;
    flex-direction: row;
  }

  .item {
    width: 100px;
    text-align: center;
    color: white;
    font-size: 2rem;
  }

  .one {
    background: blue;
  }

  .two {
    background: red;
  }

  .three {
    background: green;
  }
</style>

<div class="container">
  <div class="item one">1</div>
  <div class="item two">2</div>
  <div class="item three">3</div>
</div>
```

Figure 10-7 shows the resulting layout. The items do not grow, and there is extra space in the container.

Figure 10-7. *The rendered result*

This behavior can be controlled with the flex-grow property, which is set on the flex item rather than the container. By default, this is 0, which means the items won't grow at all. flex-grow is a relative measure. If all of the items are set to flex-grow: 1, they will all grow equally to fill the space. Let's do that in Listing 10-6.

Listing 10-6. Adding the flex-grow property

```
<style>
  .container {
    border: 1px solid black;
    padding: 0.5rem;
    width: 500px;
    display: flex;
    flex-direction: row;
  }

  .item {
    width: 100px;
    text-align: center;
    color: white;
    font-size: 2rem;
    flex-grow: 1;
  }

  .one {
    background: blue;
  }

  .two {
    background: red;
  }
```

```
  .three {
    background: green;
  }
</style>

<div class="container">
  <div class="item one">1</div>
  <div class="item two">2</div>
  <div class="item three">3</div>
</div>
```

Figure 10-8 shows the resulting layout, where the flex items all grow equally to fill the available space in the container.

Figure 10-8. *The flex items grow to fill the container*

Suppose we want item 2 to grow twice as much as item 1 and item 3. We can specify different relative flex-grow values, and they will be sized accordingly. Listing 10-7 shows an example of this, setting flex-grow to 2 on the middle flex item.

Listing 10-7. Specifying different flex-grow values

```
<style>
  .container {
    border: 1px solid black;
    padding: 0.5rem;
    width: 500px;
    display: flex;
    flex-direction: row;
  }

  .item {
    width: 100px;
    text-align: center;
    color: white;
```

```
    font-size: 2rem;
    flex-grow: 1;
  }

  .one {
    background: blue;
  }

  .two {
    background: red;
    flex-grow: 2;
  }

  .three {
    background: green;
  }
</style>

<div class="container">
  <div class="item one">1</div>
  <div class="item two">2</div>
  <div class="item three">3</div>
</div>
```

The result is shown in Figure 10-9, where the middle item is larger than the others.

Figure 10-9. *Item 2 grows to take more of the available space*

You might notice that item 2 is not twice as large as items 1 and 3. Items 1 and 3 are 150px wide, and item 2 is 200px wide. Instead, item 2 takes twice as much of the available space as items 1 and 3.

All three items started at 100px. Items 1 and 3 grew by 50px, while item 2 grew by 100px – twice that of the others.

flex-shrink (item)

We saw earlier that if the flex items exceed the size of the container, the browser will try to shrink them to fit. By default, it will try to shrink all elements evenly. Just like we can control growth with flex-grow, we can also control shrinking with flex-shrink.

The flex-shrink property specifies the amount of shrinking that can be done to a flex item relative to the other items. This defaults to 1, which is why all of the elements were shrunk evenly.

Listing 10-8 specifies a flex-shrink of 2 for item 2.

Listing 10-8. Specifying a flex-shrink of 2

```
<style>
  .container {
    border: 1px solid black;
    padding: 0.5rem;
    width: 300px;
    display: flex;
    flex-direction: row;
  }

  .item {
    width: 200px;
    font-size: 2rem;
    color: white;
    text-align: center;
  }

  .one {
    background: blue;
  }

  .two {
    background: red;
    flex-shrink: 2;
  }
```

```
  .three {
    background: green;
  }
</style>

<div class="container">
  <div class="item one">1</div>
  <div class="item two">2</div>
  <div class="item three">3</div>
</div>
```

The resulting layout is shown in Figure 10-10. This time, the middle item is smaller than the others.

Figure 10-10. *Item 2 shrinks twice as much as items 1 and 3*

Each item is 200px, which means the total width taken up by the items is 600px. But the container is only 300px wide, so the items have to be shrunk. With the default flex-shrink of 1 for all items, each item would be shrunk by 100px, to be 100px wide. But because item 2 has a flex-shrink of 2, it will shrink twice as much as the others.

flex-basis (item)

The flex-basis property sets the initial size of a flex item along the main axis before flex-grow and flex-shrink factors are applied.

Alignment and spacing

So far, we've seen how to size the flex items in a flexbox layout. In this section, we'll look at alignment (what happens when all the items are not the same size in the cross axis?) and spacing (how is leftover space distributed?).

The writing mode

Some of the values for these properties depend on the *writing mode*. The writing mode is defined by the `writing-mode` property. This property determines the way block elements are laid out, and how inline elements flow inside them.

Furthermore, the way the writing mode behaves depends on the user's language. In some languages, text flows from left to right (LTR); in others, it flows from right to left (RTL).

The default value is `horizontal-tb`. For LTR languages, elements flow from left to right; for RTL languages, elements flow from right to left. Block elements and lines of text flow from top to bottom.

Other values include `vertical-rl` and `vertical-lr`. For these values, elements flow vertically from top to bottom (for LTR languages) or bottom to top (for RTL languages). With `vertical-rl`, block elements and lines of text flow from right to left (for LTR languages) or left to right (for RTL languages). Finally, with `vertical-lr`, block elements and lines of text flow from left to right (for LTR languages), or right to left (for RTL languages).

Properties

Like with sizing properties, some of these properties are applied to the flex container, and others are applied to the flex items.

justify-content (container)

The `justify-content` property, set on the container, controls how flex items are aligned/spaced along the main axis. By default, this is set to `flex-start`. This means the items are bunched together at the beginning of the main axis. The following examples demonstrate some of the commonly used values for `justify-content`, on an element with `flex-direction: row` and assuming a left-to-right language. The supported values for `justify-content` are shown in Table 10-1.

Table 10-1. *The values for the* `justify-content` *property*

Value	Description	Example
`flex-start`	Lays out all the items next to each other at the beginning of the main axis	
`flex-end`	Lays out all the items next to each other at the end of the main axis	
`center`	Lays out all the items next to each other, centered along the main axis	
`space-between`	Maximizes the space between the items. The first item is flush with the start of the main axis, the last item is flush with the end of the main axis, and the other items are distributed evenly	
`space-around`	Similar to space-between, except items have space on both ends. These spacings are not collapsed between the middle items. The end result is a smaller space before the first item and after the last item	
`space-evenly`	Similar to space-around, except the space is even on all sides of all items	

align-items (container)

The `align-items` property is also set on the container. It controls how flex items are aligned along the cross axis. The default value is `stretch`, which will stretch items along the cross axis to fill the container's size, while respecting height and width constraints. The different options for `align-items` are shown in Table 10-2.

Table 10-2. *Values of the align-items property*

Value	Description	Example
stretch	Stretches the items to fill all available space along the cross axis. An element won't be stretched beyond its height or max-height	
flex-start	Items are aligned to the start of the cross axis	
flex-end	Items are aligned to the end of the cross axis	
center	Items are aligned to the center of the cross axis	
baseline	Items are aligned along the baseline of their text	

align-content (container)

When there are multiple rows (or columns in a column flexbox layout), and there is extra space in the cross axis, align-content specifies how this space is distributed. The default is stretch, which, like with align-items, stretches the items along the cross axis. The values for align-content are shown in Table 10-3.

Table 10-3. *Values of the* align-content *property*

Value	Description	Example
stretch	Stretches the items to fill all available space along the cross axis. An element won't be stretched beyond its height or max-height	
flex-start	Aligns the rows at the beginning of the cross axis	
flex-end	Aligns the rows at the end of the cross axis	
center	Aligns the rows at the center of the cross axis	
space-between	Maximizes the spacing between the rows	
space-around	Spacing around the rows, with half spaces at the beginning and end	
space-evenly	Equal spacing around all the rows	

`align-self` (item)

The align-items property applies the alignment to all of the flex items, but an individual item can specify its own individual alignment that overrides what was set on the container with the `align-self` property.

The `order` property

By default, items are laid out according to two factors:

- The order they occur in the HTML

- The value of the `flex-direction` property

This ordering can be changed by using the `order` property on flex items. This property, when set on a flex item, defines the order in which it appears.

Multiple flex items can have the same value for the `order` property. If more than one item has the same order, those items will be laid out in the order they appear in the source HTML.

Accessibility tip

The `order` property only affects the displayed order on screen. It does not affect the order of the elements in other contexts. A screen reader, for example, will read the elements in their source order, not the displayed order.

This makes the display of the items out of sync from how they are displayed on screen, which could be confusing. For this reason, the `order` property is best used sparingly.

Examples

The following sections show some examples of what can be achieved with a flexbox layout.

Absolute centering

With flexbox, the problem of absolute (horizontal and vertical) centering is easily solved by setting both `align-items` and `justify-content` to center. We do this in Listing 10-9.

Listing 10-9. Absolute centering with flexbox

```
<style>
  .container {
    background: skyblue;
    display: flex;
    align-items: center;
    justify-content: center;
    width: 10rem;
    height: 10rem;
  }

  .item {
    background: orangered;
    width: 5rem;
    height: 5rem;
  }
</style>

<div class="container">
  <div class="item"></div>
</div>
```

The resulting layout is shown in Figure 10-11, where the inner box is horizontally and vertically centered within the outer box.

Figure 10-11. *The inner box is centered on both the main axis and cross axis*

Page layout

Nesting flexbox layouts allows you to create all kinds of layouts. Listing 10-10 has an example of a full-page layout using flexbox.

Listing 10-10. A full-page layout with flexbox

```
<style>
  body {
    margin: 0;
  }

  .container {
    display: flex;
    flex-direction: column;
    height: 100vh;
    border: 5px dashed black;
    box-sizing: border-box;
  }

  .header {
    background: skyblue;
    padding: 1rem;
  }
```

```css
  .main {
    display: flex;
    flex-direction: row;
    flex-grow: 1;
    border: 5px dashed blue;
  }

  .sidebar {
    background: cornflowerblue;
    padding: 1rem;
  }

  .content {
    flex-grow: 1;
    background: beige;
    padding: 1rem;
  }

  .sidebar-2 {
    background: turquoise;
    padding: 1rem;
  }

  .footer {
    background: orange;
    padding: 1rem;
  }
</style>

<div class="container">
  <header class="header">Header</header>
  <main class="main">
    <div class="sidebar">Sidebar</div>
    <div class="content">Content</div>
    <div class="sidebar-2">Sidebar 2</div>
  </main>
  <footer class="footer">Footer</footer>
</div>
```

The resulting full-page layout is shown in Figure 10-12.

Figure 10-12. *The flexbox layout*

The root container defines a `column` flexbox layout (the black border). It contains a header, a main element which contains the other content (the blue border), and a footer. The main element gets a `flex-grow` of 1. This means that while the header and footer use just enough space for their content, the main element will grow to fill the remaining space.

Then, the main element has a `row` flexbox layout. The two sidebars on either end just use their natural width, and the content area in the middle again uses a `flex-grow` of 1 to fill horizontally.

We could have even deeper nesting. For example, the header could contain a `row` flexbox layout with navigation links, or the sidebar could contain a `column` flexbox layout.

Summary

In this chapter, we learned all about flexbox layouts:

- A flexbox layout is made up of a flex container and its flex items.

- A flexbox layout is one-dimensional; it is either a single row or a single column.

- A flex container is created by setting `display` to `flex` or `inline-flex`.

- A flex container has a direction and two axes, the main axis and the cross axis.

- Flex containers can be nested inside other flex containers.

- Flexbox can be used to absolutely center an element inside its container.

CHAPTER 11

Responsive Design

Responsive design is a technique for designing page layouts so that they are usable on devices with a variety of different screen sizes. Media queries are one of the main tools used for responsive design, as are flexbox and CSS Grid.

A layout that looks good on a high-resolution desktop display might not look so good on an iPhone. *Media queries* allow you to apply different CSS rules, or even entire style sheets, depending on the size of the viewport.

Media queries have other uses, too. For example, you can apply a different set of styles for when a page is printed than when it is displayed on a screen by using the print medium.

The `viewport` meta tag

In order for a site to look correctly on mobile devices, you will need to add the `viewport` meta tag to your HTML inside the head element:

```
<meta
  name="viewport"
  content="width=device-width, initial-scale=1.0">
```

This tells the browser how to set the page's dimensions and zoom level. The typical value used for width is `device-width`; however, this could also be set to an explicit pixel width as well.

© Joe Attardi 2020
J. Attardi, *Modern CSS*, https://doi.org/10.1007/978-1-4842-6294-8_11

Media queries

A media query is defined as an at-rule, @media. It specifies a medium (all, print, screen, or speech) and a condition. If no medium is specified, it defaults to all. If the condition is met, the CSS rules inside the block are applied to the document. If it is not met, the CSS rules are ignored.

Listing 11-1 has an example of a media query.

Listing 11-1. An example media query

```
h1 {
  color: red;
}

@media screen and (max-width: 400px) {
  h1 {
    color: blue;
  }
}
```

In a viewport that has a width of 400px or less, h1 elements will be blue. Otherwise, they will be red. Media queries are constantly being evaluated and styles conditionally applied. They aren't only calculated when the page first loads. You can test the given CSS by opening the page using it and notice the h1 elements are red. If you resize the window to below 400px, the h1 elements will change from red to blue. Resize the screen back above 400px, and they will turn red again.

With responsive design, the min-width and max-width rules are commonly used, as they are good indicators of viewport size. There are many other media query rules. For example, this rule will apply only when the user's device is in landscape orientation:

```
@media (orientation: landscape)
```

Some queries are based on physical attributes of the device (such as width or orientation), but others are based on settings the user has configured in their operating system. In Chapter 9, we saw the prefers-reduced-motion query. Another example of a preference-based query is prefers-color-scheme. On platforms that support "dark mode," such as macOS, this can be used to query if the user is using dark mode:

```
@media (prefers-color-scheme: dark)
```

Media queries also support logical operators such as and, or, and not:

```
@media screen
  and (min-width: 600px)
  and (orientation: landscape)
```

The only operator is also supported. Using only assures that a media query's rules are not applied on older browsers that don't understand the full query.

Media queries can also be used to conditionally load an entire style sheet. For example, you may want to apply an entirely different style sheet if the page is being printed using the HTML in Listing 11-2.

Listing 11-2. Conditionally loading style sheets

```
<link rel="stylesheet"
      href="style.css"
      media="screen">
<link rel="stylesheet"
      href="print.css"
      media="print">
```

Breakpoints

A *breakpoint* is the threshold at which a page's layout will change due to the viewport size with a media query. Defining your breakpoints is not an exact science, as there are many different devices in use today, all with different screen sizes. It's better to set breakpoints based on the *content*. That is, you should try to avoid targeting specific devices with media queries. Instead, experiment with different viewport sizes, and find the points where your layout and design start looking cramped. Then you know where to set your breakpoints.

Figure 11-1 shows an example layout, with a viewport width of 1,000 pixels.

Today's Top Headlines

Lorem ipsum dolor sit amet, consectetur adipiscing elit. Fusce aliquam, magna vitae rhoncus ornare, ipsum erat convallis ligula, eu fermentum neque eros vitae tortor. Integer eleifend dolor ut leo vehicula, ut facilisis arcu tristique. Quisque porta auctor risus, et tristique mauris vehicula quis. In feugiat mauris vel purus ultrices ornare. Nunc tincidunt velit a mi tincidunt pellentesque. Integer lobortis dictum lacinia. Vivamus sed faucibus eros. Proin at dignissim sapien. Sed ac tincidunt massa.

Figure 11-1. *An example layout*

The only CSS that has been applied is that the h1 element at the top has been set to a font-size of 5rem.

If we start to shrink the viewport, we'll see that the heading text wraps at around 785 pixels, as shown in Figure 11-2.

Today's Top Headlines

Lorem ipsum dolor sit amet, consectetur adipiscing elit. Fusce aliquam, magna vitae rhoncus ornare, ipsum erat convallis ligula, eu fermentum neque eros vitae tortor. Integer eleifend dolor ut leo vehicula, ut facilisis arcu tristique. Quisque porta auctor risus, et tristique mauris vehicula quis. In feugiat mauris vel purus ultrices ornare. Nunc tincidunt velit a mi tincidunt pellentesque. Integer lobortis dictum lacinia. Vivamus sed faucibus eros. Proin at dignissim sapien. Sed ac tincidunt massa.

Figure 11-2. *The heading text wrapped*

The headline takes up a lot of vertical space now, so this might be a good place for a breakpoint. We can make its font smaller when the viewport is 785 pixels or less by using the media query in Listing 11-3.

Listing 11-3. Applying a media query to make the heading font smaller

```
@media screen and (max-width: 785px) {
  h1 {
    font-size: 3rem;
  }
}
```

Figure 11-3 shows the resulting layout. Now when we view the site at that viewport size, the heading is smaller and takes up less vertical space, since it doesn't wrap.

Today's Top Headlines

Lorem ipsum dolor sit amet, consectetur adipiscing elit. Fusce aliquam, magna vitae rhoncus ornare, ipsum erat convallis ligula, eu fermentum neque eros vitae tortor. Integer eleifend dolor ut leo vehicula, ut facilisis arcu tristique. Quisque porta auctor risus, et tristique mauris vehicula quis. In feugiat mauris vel purus ultrices ornare. Nunc tincidunt velit a mi tincidunt pellentesque. Integer lobortis dictum lacinia. Vivamus sed faucibus eros. Proin at dignissim sapien. Sed ac tincidunt massa.

Figure 11-3.   *The heading text is smaller at this viewport size*

This will result in more content being visible on devices with a smaller viewport. If we start resizing the viewport again, we'll find that the heading is wrapping again at around 480 pixels, as shown in Figure 11-4.

Today's Top Headlines

Lorem ipsum dolor sit amet, consectetur adipiscing elit. Fusce aliquam, magna vitae rhoncus ornare, ipsum erat convallis ligula, eu fermentum neque eros vitae tortor. Integer eleifend dolor ut leo vehicula, ut facilisis arcu tristique. Quisque porta auctor risus, et tristique mauris vehicula quis. In feugiat mauris vel purus ultrices ornare. Nunc tincidunt velit a mi tincidunt pellentesque. Integer lobortis dictum lacinia. Vivamus sed faucibus eros. Proin at dignissim sapien. Sed ac tincidunt massa.

Figure 11-4.   *The heading is wrapping again*

We can specify another breakpoint here to again prevent the heading from wrapping in Listing 11-4.

Listing 11-4. Adding another media query

```
@media screen and (max-width: 785px) {
  h1 {
    font-size: 3rem;
  }
}

@media screen and (max-width: 480px) {
  h1 {
    font-size: 2rem;
  }
}
```

The result is shown in Figure 11-5, where the heading text is very small.

Today's Top Headlines

Lorem ipsum dolor sit amet, consectetur adipiscing elit. Fusce aliquam, magna vitae rhoncus ornare, ipsum erat convallis ligula, eu fermentum neque eros vitae tortor. Integer eleifend dolor ut leo vehicula, ut facilisis arcu tristique. Quisque porta auctor risus, et tristique mauris vehicula quis. In feugiat mauris vel purus ultrices ornare. Nunc tincidunt velit a mi tincidunt pellentesque. Integer lobortis dictum lacinia. Vivamus sed faucibus eros. Proin at dignissim sapien. Sed ac tincidunt massa.

Figure 11-5. *The heading text gets even smaller at this viewport size*

At this breakpoint, the image looks really big compared to the heading size. We can make the image a little smaller at this breakpoint inside the same media query. This is done in Listing 11-5.

Listing 11-5. Adjusting the image size

```
@media screen and (max-width: 785px) {
  h1 {
    font-size: 3rem;
  }
}

@media screen and (max-width: 480px) {
  h1 {
    font-size: 2rem;
  }

  img {
    width: 250px;
  }
}
```

The resulting layout is shown in Figure 11-6, where the image is smaller.

Today's Top Headlines

Lorem ipsum dolor sit amet, consectetur adipiscing elit. Fusce aliquam, magna vitae rhoncus ornare, ipsum erat convallis ligula, eu fermentum neque eros vitae tortor. Integer eleifend dolor ut leo vehicula, ut facilisis arcu tristique. Quisque porta auctor risus, et tristique mauris vehicula quis. In feugiat mauris vel purus ultrices ornare. Nunc tincidunt velit a mi tincidunt pellentesque. Integer lobortis dictum lacinia. Vivamus sed faucibus eros. Proin at dignissim sapien. Sed ac tincidunt massa.

Figure 11-6. *The image is smaller at this viewport size*

Now, the image looks better sized relative to the rest of the content.

Responsive layouts with flexbox

Some responsive layouts can be achieved without even using media queries. For example, we can use the flex-wrap property on a flex container to automatically wrap elements to the next line if the viewport is too narrow, in order to prevent the need for horizontal scrolling. Listing 11-6 contains an example flexbox layout.

Listing 11-6. An example layout

```
<style>
  .container {
    display: flex;
    flex-direction: row;
    justify-content: center;
    background: skyblue;
    padding: 0.25rem;
  }

  .item {
    background: red;
    color: white;
    text-align: center;
    margin: 0.25rem;
    font-size: 2rem;
  }

  .wide {
    width: 300px;
  }
</style>

<div class="container">
  <div class="item">Flex Item 1</div>
  <div class="item wide">Flex Item 2</div>
  <div class="item">Flex Item 3</div>
```

```
  <div class="item">Flex Item 4</div>
  <div class="item wide">Flex Item 5</div>
  <div class="item">Flex Item 6</div>
</div>
```

With a wide enough viewport, this results in the layout shown in Figure 11-7.

Figure 11-7. *The rendered layout with a wide viewport*

This looks pretty good. Let's see how this looks with a narrower viewport, shown in Figure 11-8.

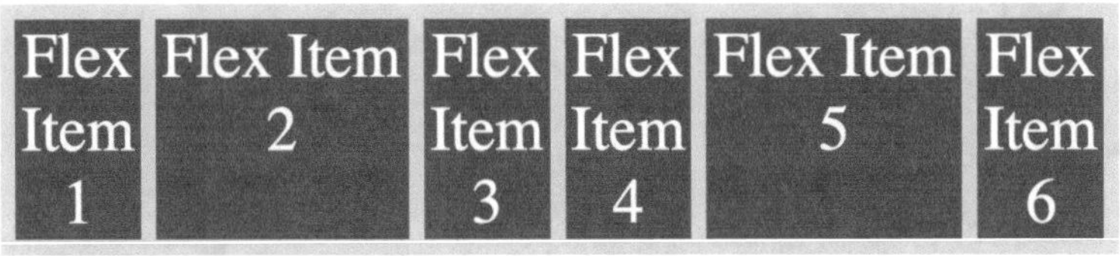

Figure 11-8. *The layout with a narrower viewport*

Now it's looking a little cramped. Let's go even narrower, like if we were viewing this layout on a mobile device, shown in Figure 11-9.

Figure 11-9. *The layout with an even narrower viewport*

The flex items have shrunk as much as possible, but the viewport still isn't wide enough, so the first and last items get cut off. We can easily solve this problem by setting flex-wrap to wrap on the container. This is shown in Listing 11-7.

Listing 11-7. Adding flex-wrap: wrap

```
<style>
  .container {
    display: flex;
    flex-direction: row;
    justify-content: center;
    flex-wrap: wrap;
    background: skyblue;
    padding: 0.25rem;
  }

  .item {
    background: red;
    color: white;
    text-align: center;
    margin: 0.25rem;
    font-size: 2rem;
  }

  .wide {
    width: 300px;
  }
</style>

<div class="container">
  <div class="item">Flex Item 1</div>
  <div class="item wide">Flex Item 2</div>
  <div class="item">Flex Item 3</div>
  <div class="item">Flex Item 4</div>
  <div class="item wide">Flex Item 5</div>
  <div class="item">Flex Item 6</div>
</div>
```

The resulting layout is shown in Figure 11-10, where the layout items now wrap.

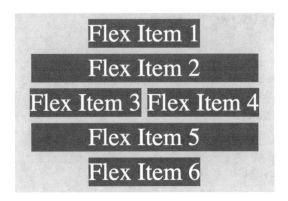

Figure 11-10.   *The wrapped layout with a narrow viewport*

Now, it looks much better in the narrow viewport. If we go even narrower, the layout will change to accommodate the new size, as shown in Figure 11-11.

Figure 11-11.   *The layout on an even narrower viewport*

Fluid typography

Earlier, we saw how to leverage media queries to adjust the font size as the viewport size changes. With fluid typography, it's possible to automatically scale the font size to viewport size without having to use media queries.

Earlier in the book, we discussed the vw unit, which is equal to 1% of the viewport width. We can use vw to specify a font size as a proportion of the viewport width. For example, for a 1,000-pixel-wide viewport, 1vw is equal to 10px. Suppose that we want our header to have a font size of 48px for a 1,000-pixel-wide viewport. We can specify the font-size as 4.8vw. Figure 11-12 shows what that looks like.

Today's Top Headlines

Lorem ipsum dolor sit amet, consectetur adipiscing elit. Fusce aliquam, magna vitae rhoncus ornare, ipsum erat convallis ligula, eu fermentum neque eros vitae tortor. Integer eleifend dolor ut leo vehicula, ut facilisis arcu tristique. Quisque porta auctor risus, et tristique mauris vehicula quis. In feugiat mauris vel purus ultrices ornare. Nunc tincidunt velit a mi tincidunt pellentesque. Integer lobortis dictum lacinia. Vivamus sed faucibus eros. Proin at dignissim sapien. Sed ac tincidunt massa.

Praesent rhoncus tortor id nisl porta, vel tempus odio venenatis. Fusce sit amet leo sagittis ante feugiat pulvinar quis vitae lacus. Vivamus odio elit, venenatis vel elit sit amet, iaculis posuere nisl. Aenean tempus velit eu dolor molestie, vitae sagittis est sollicitudin. Aliquam congue dui id eros tincidunt egestas. Praesent ut metus maximus, porttitor erat sit amet, molestie nibh. Ut urna orci, vulputate at felis consequat, vehicula mollis magna. Curabitur quis hendrerit tellus. Class aptent taciti sociosqu ad litora torquent per conubia nostra, per inceptos himenaeos. Vivamus varius quam quis nibh ullamcorper volutpat.

Figure 11-12. *Using a variable font size proportional to the viewport width*

However, there's a problem. If the viewport becomes very wide, the font size of the heading becomes very large – at a viewport size of 2,000 pixels, the font size becomes 96px. Look at the font size of the heading in Figure 11-13 compared to the body text size.

Today's Top Headlines

Lorem ipsum dolor sit amet, consectetur adipiscing elit. Fusce aliquam, magna vitae rhoncus ornare, ipsum erat convallis ligula, eu fermentum neque eros vitae tortor. Integer eleifend dolor ut leo vehicula, ut facilisis arcu tristique. Quisque porta auctor risus, et tristique mauris vehicula quis. In feugiat mauris vel purus ultrices ornare. Nunc tincidunt velit a mi tincidunt pellentesque. Integer lobortis dictum lacinia. Vivamus sed faucibus eros. Proin at dignissim sapien. Sed ac tincidunt massa.

Praesent rhoncus tortor id nisl porta, vel tempus odio venenatis. Fusce sit amet leo sagittis ante feugiat pulvinar quis vitae lacus. Vivamus odio elit, venenatis vel elit sit amet, iaculis posuere nisl. Aenean tempus velit eu dolor molestie, vitae sagittis est sollicitudin. Aliquam congue dui id eros tincidunt egestas. Praesent ut metus maximus, porttitor erat sit amet, molestie nibh. Ut urna orci, vulputate at felis consequat, vehicula mollis magna. Curabitur quis hendrerit tellus. Class aptent taciti sociosqu ad litora torquent per conubia nostra, per inceptos himenaeos. Vivamus varius quam quis nibh ullamcorper volutpat.

Figure 11-13. *A very large font size*

On the other extreme, if the viewport is very narrow, the heading's font size becomes very small – almost as small as the body text, shown in Figure 11-14.

Today's Top Headlines

Lorem ipsum dolor sit amet, consectetur adipiscing elit. Fusce aliquam, magna vitae rhoncus ornare, ipsum erat convallis ligula, eu fermentum neque eros vitae tortor. Integer eleifend dolor ut leo vehicula, ut facilisis arcu tristique. Quisque porta auctor risus, et tristique mauris vehicula quis. In feugiat mauris vel purus ultrices ornare. Nunc tincidunt velit a mi tincidunt pellentesque. Integer lobortis dictum lacinia. Vivamus sed faucibus eros. Proin at dignissim sapien. Sed ac tincidunt massa.

Figure 11-14.   The heading font is very small for a narrow viewport

The `clamp` function

We can fix this by using the `clamp` function. `clamp` takes three arguments: the minimum size, the preferred size, and the maximum size. We can keep our font size of `4.8vw` as the preferred size and add a lower bound of `48px` and an upper bound of `64px`:

```
font-size: clamp(48px, 4.8vw, 64px);
```

Now the font size adjusts automatically with the viewport width as before, but now it will never drop below `48px` or go above `64px`.

Responsive images

Previously, we used a media query to change the size of an image if the viewport was narrower than a certain threshold. There is another technique we can use that allows images to scale with the viewport width without using media queries.

Figure 11-15 shows our layout from before, using an image that is 800 pixels wide.

Today's Top Headlines

Figure 11-15. *An 800 pixel wide image*

It looks good at this width, but what happens if the viewport is less than 800 pixels wide? This is illustrated in Figure 11-16.

Today's Top Headlines

Figure 11-16. *The image with a viewport width of less than 800 pixels*

At this viewport size, the image is cut off and requires horizontal scrolling to view the rest of it. We can change this behavior so that the image resizes along with the viewport (or its container) with two CSS properties:

```
img {
  max-width: 100%;
  height: auto;
}
```

This sets the image so that its width never exceeds the width of its container. The `height: auto` makes sure that the image retains its aspect ratio.

Now, as we resize the viewport, the image is resized and maintains the proper aspect ratio, as shown in Figure 11-17.

Figure 11-17. *The image now resizes with the viewport*

After making these changes, the CSS for our responsive page is very simple, shown in Listing 11-8.

Listing 11-8. The final CSS for this layout

```
img {
  max-width: 100%;
  height: auto;
}

h1 {
  font-size: clamp(48px, 4.8vw, 64px);
}
```

Adapting a layout with media queries

There are still good use cases for media queries with responsive design, however. Let's look at the page layout in Listing 11-9.

Listing 11-9. A page layout

```
<style>
  body {
    margin: 0;
  }

  .container {
    display: flex;
    flex-direction: column;
    height: 100vh;
  }

  .header {
    background: orange;
    padding: 1rem;
  }

  .main {
    display: flex;
    flex-direction: row;
    flex-grow: 1;
  }

  .content {
    background: salmon;
    padding: 1rem;
    flex-grow: 1;
  }

  .sidebar {
    display: flex;
    flex-direction: column;
    background: skyblue;
    padding: 1rem;
  }
```

```
  .sidebar a {
    margin: 1rem;
    padding: 0.5rem 2rem;
    border: 1px solid black;
  }

  .sidebar2 {
    background: lime;
    padding: 1rem;
  }

  .footer {
    background: beige;
    padding: 1rem;
  }
</style>

<div class="container">
  <header class="header">Header</header>
  <main class="main">
    <nav class="sidebar">
      <a href="/home">Home</a>
      <a href="/about">About</a>
      <a href="/photos">Photos</a>
    </nav>
    <div class="content">
      Hello world!
    </div>
    <div class="sidebar2">
      Sidebar 2
    </div>
  </main>
  <footer class="footer">Footer</footer>
</div>
```

This results in the layout shown in Figure 11-18.

Figure 11-18. *The rendered layout*

If we decrease the viewport width, the main content area gets squashed between the two sidebars, as seen in Figure 11-19.

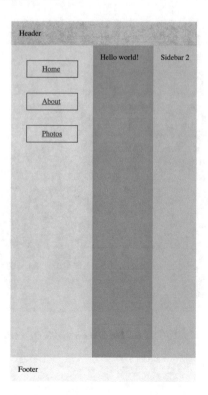

Figure 11-19. *The narrow layout*

We can improve this by adding a media query and making a few overrides. Let's set the breakpoint at 700 pixels. Below this threshold, we'll change the main element to have a flex-direction of column rather than row. This will stack the three regions vertically, allowing them each to take up the full width of the container. The media query is shown in Listing 11-10.

Listing 11-10. Adding a media query to the main element

```
@media screen and (max-width: 700px) {
  .main {
    flex-direction: column;
  }
}
```

Now the content takes up the full width and is no longer constrained horizontally, as shown in Figure 11-20. The new layout takes effect at 700 pixels or less.

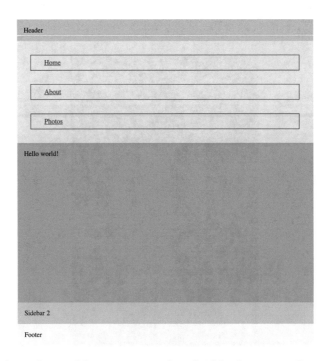

Figure 11-20. *The adjusted layout at its threshold of 700 pixels*

The navigation is taking up a lot of vertical space now, though. We can add another override inside the media query, shown in Listing 11-11, to change the navigation links to be horizontal.

Listing 11-11. Adding another override

```
@media screen and (max-width: 700px) {
  .main {
    flex-direction: column;
  }

  .sidebar {
    flex-direction: row;
    justify-content: center;
  }
}
```

The resulting layout is shown in Figure 11-21.

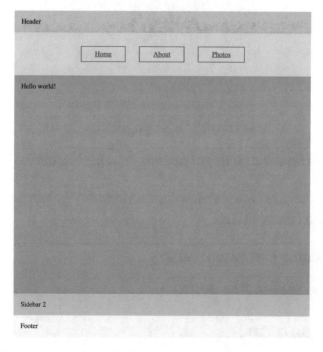

Figure 11-21. *The navigation links laid out horizontally*

This responsive layout looks a lot better with a narrower viewport. But this is still a wider viewport than that of a mobile device. Let's shrink it down further, to 350 pixels, in Figure 11-22.

Figure 11-22.   *The layout as it might appear on a mobile device*

Now the navigation links are overflowing the viewport. We can fix this by setting flex-wrap to wrap in Listing 11-12.

Listing 11-12.   Adding flex-wrap: wrap

```
@media screen and (max-width: 700px) {
  .main {
    flex-direction: column;
  }
```

```
.sidebar {
    flex-direction: row;
    justify-content: center;
    flex-wrap: wrap;
  }
}
```

In Figure 11-23, we can see that the navigation links now wrap.

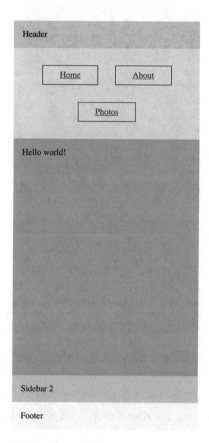

Figure 11-23. *The wrapped navigation links*

This looks better – the navigation links no longer overflow the viewport. There are still some other ways we could improve on this design. For example, at the narrow viewport size, we could replace the navigation links with a dropdown or popup menu. This would probably involve some JavaScript and DOM manipulation for toggling the menu.

We could also try to get this to fit on one line by making the navigation links smaller, removing the padding, as shown in Figure 11-24. This would work, but would probably be frustrating for mobile users, as the touch targets on the screen would be very small.

Figure 11-24. *The layout with smaller links, which are not ideal for mobile*

In this instance, the best option would probably be to add a menu of some kind in place of the navigation links on a narrow viewport like on a mobile device.

Summary

We have seen just a few of the tools at your disposal to adapt your layouts and designs to different screen sizes:

- Media queries allow CSS rules to be applied conditionally.

- A breakpoint is a threshold used in a media query, where there is a layout change.

- An element's font size can be proportional to the width of the viewport and limited by using the `clamp` function.

- Sometimes, only minor changes are needed inside a media query, such as setting `flex-wrap` to `wrap` or the `flex-direction` from `row` to `column` in a flex container.

- Images can automatically resize to the viewport by setting `max-width` to 100% and `height` to `auto`.

CHAPTER 12

CSS Grid

We've looked at flexbox layouts in depth and have seen how powerful they can be. Still, there are limitations. Flexbox is a one-dimensional layout where items are arranged horizontally or vertically in rows or columns.

CSS Grid is a relatively new feature that allows you to create two-dimensional grid layouts with rows and columns. It is the most powerful layout system available with CSS today. CSS Grid enjoys wide browser support – even IE11 supports it, although its support is only partial and uses an older version of the specification.

Basic concepts

Let's start with the basic concepts of CSS Grid.

Grid container

The *grid container* is the outer element that contains the grid layout. All of its direct children are grid items. To make an element a grid container, set its `display` property to `grid` or `inline-grid`. The difference is an element with `display: grid` will be a block element, where an element with `display: inline-grid` will be an inline element.

Grid item

All immediate children of the grid container are *grid items*. Beyond the immediate children, descendant elements are not grid items. No special CSS properties need to be applied to make an item a grid item. The child elements automatically become grid items, and by default they are laid out in the order that they appear in the HTML markup.

© Joe Attardi 2020
J. Attardi, *Modern CSS*, https://doi.org/10.1007/978-1-4842-6294-8_12

Grid lines

Grid lines divide the rows and columns of the grid (Figure 12-1). The grid lines are numbered starting with 1.

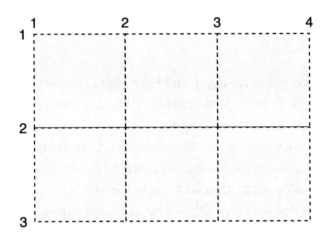

Figure 12-1. *Grid lines*

Grid tracks

The *tracks* of the grid are the rows and columns between the grid lines. The tracks are what contain the grid items. Like with grid lines, the numbering of tracks starts at 1. In Figure 12-2, row track 1 is highlighted.

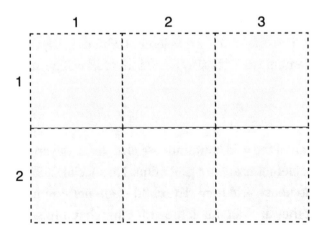

Figure 12-2. *Grid tracks*

Grid areas

A grid area is the space enclosed by any four grid lines. It can contain a single cell or multiple cells. A 4x4 grid area is highlighted in Figure 12-3.

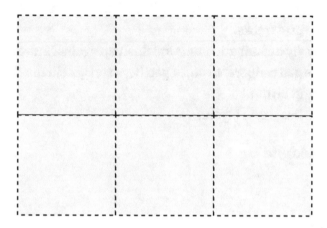

Figure 12-3. *A grid area*

Explicit grid

When grid rows and columns are explicitly defined with CSS properties, this is known as the *explicit grid*.

Implicit grid

If more items are added than are accounted for in the explicit grid, the grid layout creates additional rows and/or columns to fit these extra items. This is the *implicit grid*.

The **fr** unit

Grid sizes can be specified with any of the units we've looked at so far – px, em, rem, even percentages. CSS Grid introduces a new unit, the fr unit. This is a fractional unit that refers to a fraction of the free space. For example, if there are four columns each at a width of 1fr, then each column will take up 25% of the total width of the grid.

Basic grids

To set up the rows and columns of the explicit grid, the `grid-template-rows` and `grid-template-columns` properties are used. These are used to specify the widths of the rows and the heights of the columns, respectively. Technically speaking, they are used to specify the size of the grid tracks.

Like with flexbox, by default grid items are flush up against one another. With grid items, we can use the gap property to add a gap between grid items. This can help us better visualize the grid layout.

Listing 12-1 has a basic grid layout.

Listing 12-1. A basic grid

```
<style>
  .container {
    display: grid;
    grid-template-columns: 10rem 10rem;
    grid-template-rows: 5rem 5rem;
    gap: 5px;
  }

  .item {
    background: lightgray;
    text-align: center;
  }
</style>

<div class="container">
  <div class="item">1</div>
  <div class="item">2</div>
  <div class="item">3</div>
  <div class="item">4</div>
</div>
```

This results in the grid layout shown in Figure 12-4.

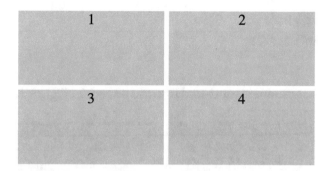

Figure 12-4. *The rendered grid*

We have defined an explicit grid with two 10rem column tracks and two 5rem row tracks. As you can see, you don't need to specify a row or column in the grid – by default, the grid container places its children in order, starting at the first column of the first row.

Right now, we have two rows and two columns – a total of four items. What happens if we add more children to the container? Let's add some more children in Listing 12-2.

Listing 12-2. Adding two more grid items

```
<style>
  .container {
    display: grid;
    grid-template-columns: 10rem 10rem;
    grid-template-rows: 5rem 5rem;
    gap: 5px;
  }

  .item {
    background: lightgray;
    text-align: center;
  }
</style>

<div class="container">
  <div class="item">1</div>
  <div class="item">2</div>
  <div class="item">3</div>
  <div class="item">4</div>
```

```
  <div class="item">5</div>
  <div class="item">6</div>
</div>
```

This results in the somewhat odd-looking grid shown in Figure 12-5.

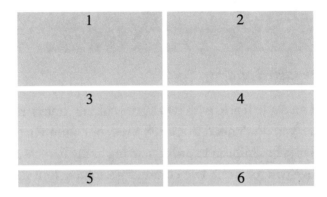

Figure 12-5. *The rendered grid*

We see items 5 and 6 in the grid. These items are in the implicit grid. Also notice that they are automatically sized to fit their content. This is the default behavior for implicit grid items. This behavior can be controlled with the `grid-auto-rows` property, where we specify the sizing for implicit grid rows. An example of this is shown in Listing 12-3.

Listing 12-3. Specifying `grid-auto-rows`

```
<style>
  .container {
    display: grid;
    grid-template-columns: 10rem 10rem;
    grid-template-rows: 5rem 5rem;
    grid-auto-rows: 5rem;
    gap: 5px;
  }

  .item {
    background: lightgray;
    text-align: center;
  }
</style>
```

```
<div class="container">
  <div class="item">1</div>
  <div class="item">2</div>
  <div class="item">3</div>
  <div class="item">4</div>
  <div class="item">5</div>
  <div class="item">6</div>
</div>
```

The resulting grid layout is shown in Figure 12-6.

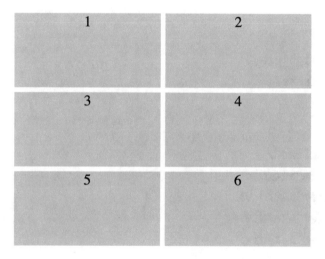

Figure 12-6. *The rendered grid*

Now, all of the grid items are the same size.

Grid sizing

Let's look at grid sizing in more detail, starting with the fr unit.

Using the **fr** unit

Listing 12-4 adapts the previous example to use the fr unit for grid sizing.

Listing 12-4. Using the fr unit

```
<style>
  .container {
    display: grid;
    grid-template-columns: 1fr 1fr 1fr;
    grid-template-rows: 5rem 5rem;
    grid-auto-rows: 5rem;
    gap: 5px;
    width: 30rem;
  }

  .item {
    background: lightgray;
    text-align: center;
  }
</style>

<div class="container">
  <div class="item">1</div>
  <div class="item">2</div>
  <div class="item">3</div>
  <div class="item">4</div>
  <div class="item">5</div>
  <div class="item">6</div>
</div>
```

The resulting grid layout is shown in Figure 12-7.

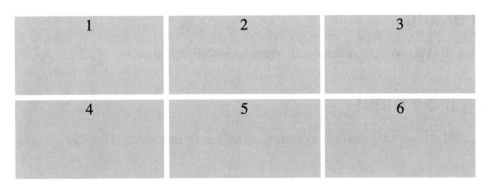

Figure 12-7. *The grid using the fr unit*

Each of the three columns is set to 1fr. This means the free space will be divided evenly between all three columns. If we set the middle column to 2fr, it would be twice as wide as the other columns, as shown in Figure 12-8.

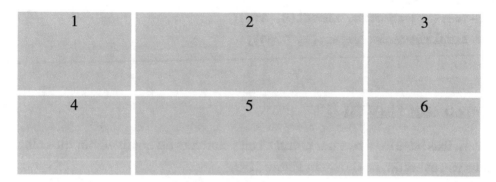

Figure 12-8. *The middle column using 2fr*

We can mix fr units with other units as well, as shown in Listing 12-5.

Listing 12-5. Mixing units

```
.container {
  display: grid;
  grid-template-columns: 200px 1fr 5rem;
  grid-template-rows: 5rem 5rem;
}
```

The **repeat** function

Sometimes, defining grid sizes can be repetitive, as seen in Listing 12-6.

Listing 12-6. A repetitive grid definition

```
.container {
  display: grid;
  grid-template-columns: 1fr 1fr 1fr 1fr;
  grid-template-rows: 5rem;
}
```

For these cases, we can use the repeat function, demonstrated in Listing 12-7.

Listing 12-7. Using the repeat function

```
.container {
  display: grid;
  grid-template-columns: repeat(4, 1fr);
  grid-template-rows: repeat(2, 5rem);
}
```

The minmax function

If we use a fixed size for a row track, and a cell's contents do not fit within the cell, the contents will overflow, as shown in Figure 12-9.

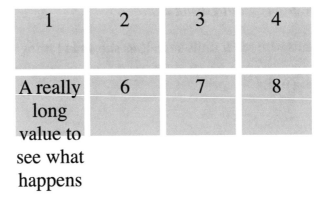

Figure 12-9. *Overflowing cell content*

To fix this scenario, we can use the minmax function. The function takes two arguments – the minimum size of the track and the maximum size. This is demonstrated in Listing 12-8.

Listing 12-8. The minmax function

```
.container {
  display: grid;
  grid-template-columns: repeat(4, 1fr);
  grid-template-rows: repeat(2, minmax(3rem, auto));
  gap: 5px;
  width: 15rem;
}
```

The resulting grid layout is shown in Figure 12-10.

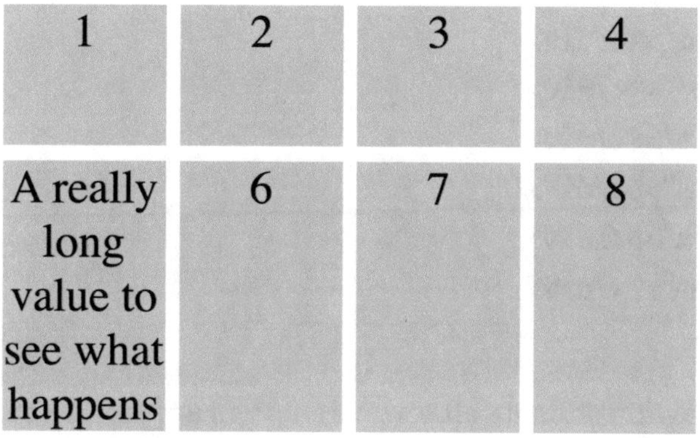

Figure 12-10. *The rendered grid*

Now the rows have a minimum height of 3rem but can grow to automatically fit the content if necessary.

auto-fill and auto-fit

Sometimes, we may not want to specify an exact number of rows or columns in a grid. For example, we may want to simply fit as many columns as will fit into the container's width. For this, we can use the auto-fill keyword in combination with the repeat function, as demonstrated in Listing 12-9.

Listing 12-9. Using the auto-fill keyword

```
<style>
  .container {
    display: grid;
    grid-template-columns: repeat(auto-fill, 5rem);
    grid-template-rows: 5rem;
    grid-auto-rows: 5rem;
    gap: 5px;
  }

  .item {
    background: lightgray;
  }
</style>
```

```
<div class="container">
  <div class="item">1</div>
  <div class="item">2</div>
  <div class="item">3</div>
  <div class="item">4</div>
  <div class="item">5</div>
  <div class="item">6</div>
  <div class="item">7</div>
</div>
```

If the viewport is wide enough, all seven items will appear in a single row, as shown in Figure 12-11.

Figure 12-11. *The grid in a wide viewport*

However, if we resize the viewport so that they don't all fit, the grid will set as many columns as will fit in the available space. The remaining grid items will wrap to the next row, as shown in Figure 12-12.

Figure 12-12. *The grid items automatically wrap with* auto-fill

auto-fill can even be combined with minmax. Let's add a border around the container from the previous example so we can better visualize the layout, shown in Figure 12-13.

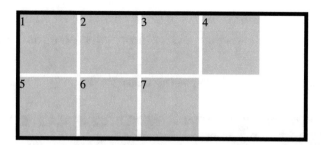

Figure 12-13. *The same example, with a border around the container*

Note the gap on the right side of the first row. This is part of the container, but there is no column there. In Listing 12-10, we add the minmax function to the column sizing.

Listing 12-10. Adding the minmax function

```
.container {
  border: 5px solid black;
  display: grid;
  grid-template-columns: repeat(
    auto-fill,
    minmax(5rem, 1fr)
  );
  grid-template-rows: 5rem;
  grid-auto-rows: 5rem;
  gap: 5px;
}
```

Now the behavior is slightly different, as shown in Figure 12-14.

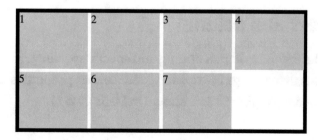

Figure 12-14. *The grid using auto-fill and minmax*

The browser is using a minimum size of 5rem. However, when there's space left over, using 1fr for each column means that each column will grow equally to use up the extra space.

Figure 12-15 shows a grid container using auto-fill.

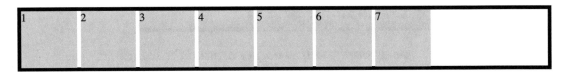

Figure 12-15. *The auto-fill behavior*

When there is more space than there are columns, with auto-fill, new columns are created which take up space in the container. With auto-fit, however, it instead sizes the items to fit within the available space *without* adding more columns. The auto-fit behavior is shown in Figure 12-16.

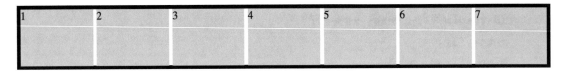

Figure 12-16. *The auto-fit behavior*

Grid positioning

By default, the grid items are placed automatically, filling each column then each row. There are options that can be used to customize the positioning of grid items.

Specifying row and column

You can override the default grid positioning and specify specific grid row and column indices for grid items using the grid-row and grid-column properties. Row and column numbers start at 1. An example of this is shown in Listing 12-11.

Listing 12-11. Specifying the row and column for an item

```
.item1 {
  background: skyblue;
  grid-row: 2;
  grid-column: 3;
}
```

The first grid item is shown in blue, in Figure 12-17.

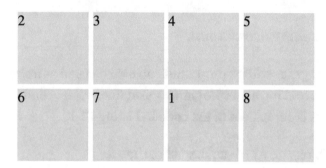

Figure 12-17. *The rendered result*

The first grid item is positioned in row 2, column 3. The rest of the grid items are automatically placed.

Spanning multiple rows or columns

A grid item can be made to span multiple rows and/or columns by using the `grid-row-start`, `grid-row-end`, `grid-column-start`, and `grid-column-end` properties. These properties reference the grid line numbers. For an item to span across column 3 and 4, it would start at line 3 and end at line 5, as demonstrated in Listing 12-12.

Listing 12-12. Using `grid-column-start` and `grid-column-end`

```
.item1 {
  background: skyblue;
  grid-row: 2;
  grid-column-start: 3;
  grid-column-end: 5;
}
```

The resulting grid layout is shown in Listing 12-18.

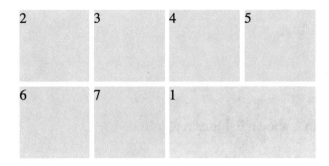

***Figure 12-18.** Spanning two columns*

The `grid-row` or `grid-column` properties can also be used as a shorthand for these properties. The expected format is the starting grid line, a slash, and the ending line. The preceding CSS block is equivalent to the code in Listing 12-13.

***Listing 12-13.** Using the `grid-column` shorthand*

```
.item1 {
  grid-row: 2;
  grid-column: 3 / 5;
}
```

Instead of specifying an ending row or column line number, we can also use the `span` keyword. This specifies that the item spans that number of rows or columns, starting at the specified start index, as shown in Listing 12-14.

***Listing 12-14.** Using the `span` keyword*

```
.item1 {
  grid-row: 2;
  grid-column: 3 / span 2;
}
```

Named grid lines

Grid lines can be referenced by their numerical index, as we have already seen. But we can also assign names to the grid lines and reference those names instead. The grid lines are named within a grid-template-rows or grid-template-columns expression, in between the grid track definitions. The grid line names are placed inside square brackets.

These grid line names can then be referenced from the grid-row and grid-column properties.

Listing 12-15 has a basic page layout defined using named grid lines.

Listing 12-15. Using named grid lines

```
<style>
  .container {
    display: grid;
    gap: 5px;
    width: 500px;
    grid-template-rows:
      [header-start] 2rem
      [content-start] 10rem
      [footer-start] 2rem
      [footer-end];
    grid-template-columns:
      [sidebar-start] 5rem
      [content-start] 1fr
      [content-end];
  }

  .container > div {
    background: lightgray;
  }

  .header {
    grid-row: header-start / content-start;
    grid-column: sidebar-start / content-end;
  }

  .footer {
    grid-column: sidebar-start / content-end;
  }
</style>
```

```
<div class="container">
  <div class="item header">Header</div>
  <div class="item sidebar">Sidebar</div>
  <div class="item content">Content</div>
  <div class="item footer">Footer</div>
</div>
```

The resulting layout is shown in Figure 12-19.

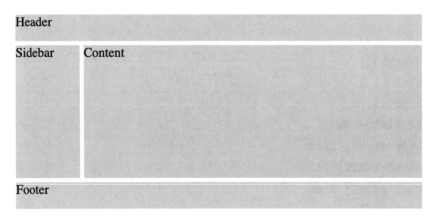

Figure 12-19. *The rendered layout*

Named grid areas

In addition to named grid lines, we can also define named grid areas. This allows us to place grid items in the desired areas without having to specify start and end lines. The areas are defined with the grid-template-areas property. If two adjacent areas have the same name, then an item placed in that area will span those areas.

grid-template-areas can also be combined with the grid sizing properties shown earlier, as demonstrated in Listing 12-16.

Listing 12-16. Specifying named grid areas

```
<style>
  .container {
    display: grid;
    grid-template-rows: 2rem 10rem 2rem;
    grid-template-columns: 5rem 1fr;
```

```
    grid-template-areas:
       'header header header'
       'sidebar content content'
       'footer footer footer';
    gap: 5px;
    width: 500px;
  }

  .header {
    grid-area: header;
  }

  .footer {
    grid-area: footer;
  }

  .sidebar {
    grid-area: sidebar;
  }

  .content {
    grid-area: content;
  }

  .container > div {
    background: lightgray;
  }
</style>

<div class="container">
  <div class="item header">Header</div>
  <div class="item sidebar">Sidebar</div>
  <div class="item content">Content</div>
  <div class="item footer">Footer</div>
</div>
```

This results in the layout shown in Figure 12-20.

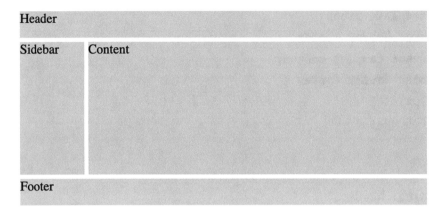

Figure 12-20. *The rendered grid layout*

Grid alignment

Just like with flexbox, CSS Grid gives you total control over the alignment of items when they don't fill their container. There are several properties that control this.

justify-items

The justify-items property defines how grid items are aligned along the row axis when there is extra space left inside a grid cell. This property is defined on the container and applies to all the items within that container. It has the following values shown in Table 12-1.

Table 12-1. *The values for the justify-items property*

Value	Description	Example
stretch	Items are stretched along the row axis to fill the entire width of the cell. This is the default	

(*continued*)

Table 12-1. (*continued*)

Value	Description	Example
start	Items are aligned with the starting edge of the cell along the row axis	
end	Items are aligned with the ending edge of the cell along the row axis	
center	Items are centered along the row axis in their cells	

align-items

The align-items property defines how grid items are aligned in the opposite direction, along the column axis. Like justify-items, this property is set on the container. Its values are listed in Table 12-2.

Table 12-2. *The values for the align-items property*

Value	Description	Example
stretch	The default value. Items are stretched along the column axis to fill the entire height of the cell	

(*continued*)

Table 12-1. (*continued*)

Value	Description	Example
start	Items are aligned at the top edge of the cell	
end	Items are aligned at the bottom edge of the cell	
center	Items are centered vertically in the cell	

justify-content

If the grid rows and/or columns aren't sized with relative/flexible units like fr, we could end up with empty space in the grid container. If this happens, the justify-content property defines where within the grid container the grid items will be aligned along the row axis. The values for justify-content are listed in Table 12-3.

Table 12-3. *The values for the* `justify-content` *property*

Value	Description	Example
`start`	Aligns the grid at the start of the row axis	
`end`	Aligns the grid at the end of the row axis	
`center`	Aligns the grid in the center of the row axis	
`stretch`	Stretches the grid columns to fill the row axis, if the columns are set to auto	
`space-around`	Adds even spacing between columns, with half-sized spaces at the start and end	
`space-evenly`	Adds even spacing between columns, with full-sized spaces at the start and end	
`space-between`	Places the first column flush with the start of the container and the last column flush with the end of the container and adds even spacing in between the other columns	

align-content

align-content is like justify-content, only it determines how the grid rows are aligned along the column axis instead of columns along the row axis. Its values are listed in Table 12-4.

Table 12-4. *The values for the* align-content *property*

Value	Description	Example
start	Aligns the grid rows at the start of the column axis	
end	Aligns the grid rows at the end of the column axis	
center	Aligns the grid rows at the center of the column axis	

(*continued*)

Table 12-4. (*continued*)

Value	Description	Example
stretch	Stretches the rows to fill the column axis, if the rows are set to auto	
space-around	Adds even spacing between rows, with half-sized spaces at the start and end	
space-evenly	Adds even spacing between rows, with full-sized spaces at the start and end	
space-between	Places the first row flush with the top of the container and the last row flush with the bottom of the container and adds even spacing in between the other rows	

Overriding for individual grid items

The justify-items and align-items properties of the grid container define the alignment of the grid items along the row and column axis, respectively. These alignments can be overridden for an individual grid item by setting the following properties on the grid item itself.

justify-self

Sets the alignment of an item inside its cell along the row axis.

align-self

Sets the alignment of an item inside its cell along the column axis.

Summary

In this chapter, we learned how to use CSS Grid:

- An element can be made a grid container by setting its display property to grid or inline-grid.

- A grid container's immediate children become grid items.

- A grid has lines, tracks, and areas.

- The explicit grid is made up of the rows and columns defined by the grid-template-rows and grid-template-columns properties.

- The implicit grid contains any elements placed after all explicit grid areas are filled.

- The fr unit uses a fraction of the available free space.

- A grid item can span multiple rows and/or columns.

- Grid lines and areas can have names. These names can then be referenced when placing grid items.

- The justify-items, align-items, justify-content, and align-content properties define how extra space is handled in grids.

- An individual grid item can override its alignment with the justify-self and align-self properties.

CHAPTER 13

Wrap Up

We have reached the end of our exploration of modern CSS. We have covered a lot of topics, starting from the basics, to layout, to transitions and animations, to more advanced layouts with flexbox and CSS Grid.

The goal of this book was to make CSS less intimidating and more accessible. I hope you have learned something of value by reading this book.

There are some other parts of the CSS ecosystem that we haven't looked at, that you should definitely look into for further learning.

CSS methodologies

As a CSS codebase grows, it can quickly get out of control. There are many solutions out there for organizing and architecting CSS code, and here are just a few of them:

- BEM (Block Element Modifier): Uses strict naming rules. Each element's name has a block, element, and modifier. An example of this is `form__button--red`. In this example `form` is the block, `button` is the element, and `red` is the modifier.

- OOCSS (Object-Oriented CSS): Applies object-oriented principles to CSS. Separates container elements, or "skins," from content.

- SMACSS (Scalable and Modular Architecture for CSS): Categorizes CSS rules into five categories: base, layout, module, state, and theme.

© Joe Attardi 2020
J. Attardi, *Modern CSS*, https://doi.org/10.1007/978-1-4842-6294-8_13

Utility-first CSS

Utility-first CSS frameworks, such as Tailwind, are fairly new but are a very different way of thinking about CSS. Instead of writing your own CSS rules that apply styles to elements, there are predefined "utility" rules that apply different types of styling. For example, using Tailwind, you might have the following:

```
<div class="p-6 bg-white rounded-lg">Hello!</div>
```

This would apply the following styles to the `div` element:

- `padding: 1.5rem` (from `p-6`)

- `background-color: white` (from `bg-white`)

- `border-radius: 0.5rem` (from `rounded-lg`)

Frameworks like Tailwind allow you to style your document without writing a single line of CSS.

Houdini

Houdini is a work-in-progress set of APIs that expose various parts of the CSS Object Model, and new APIs, to the developer. This allows for the creation of custom CSS properties, layouts, and more. Browser support is currently very limited, and some of the specifications are still at an early stage.

There are many new and exciting developments in the world of CSS on the way that will give you, the web developer, more power and control over styling your websites and apps. I hope this book has helped you chart your journey into further exploration of CSS.

Index

A

Absolutely positioned
element, 138–142
Adjacent sibling combinator, 22
Align-content
property, 222, 278, 279
Align-items property, 220, 221, 275, 276
Align-self property, 223
Animations
accessibility, 202, 203
avoid simultaneous, 201
element, 194
@keyframes rule, 193
multiple, 198, 199
property
delay, 195
direction, 197
duration, 195
fill-mode, 195–197
iteration-count, 197
name, 195
play-state, 198
timing-function, 195
Attribute selectors, 19, 20
auto-fill behavior, 268
auto-fill keyword, 265
auto-fit behavior, 268
Autoprefixer, 7

B

Backgrounds
border-box, 90
content-box, 91
images
clip property, 90
position property, 83, 85
position property, 84
repeat, 80, 82, 83
size property, 85, 86, 88, 89
lighting effect, gradient, 104
padding and changing border, 90
padding-box, 91
shorthand property, 91
Block element, 38, 39, 119, 120
Block *vs.* inline elements, 26
Border-box, 37, 90
Borders, 33
collapse property, 65, 66
color property, 64
radius, 66, 67, 69
shorthand property, 65
style property, 64
width property, 64
Border-width property, 62–64
Box model
border, 33, 35, 36
box-sizing property, 36, 37

© Joe Attardi 2020
J. Attardi, *Modern CSS*, https://doi.org/10.1007/978-1-4842-6294-8

G

H

I

Printed in the United States
By Bookmasters